ELIMINATION

THE FIRST STEP TOWARDS GROWTH

ROHHAN PATIL

Made with ♥ on the Notion Press Platform
www.notionpress.com

Contents

Acknowledgements

First and foremost, I would like to express my deepest gratitude to my family for their unwavering support throughout this journey. To my loving partner, Swagata, your encouragement, patience, and belief in me have been the foundation upon which this book was built. You've been my rock and my constant source of inspiration.

To my newborn princess, you've given me a fresh perspective on life, and the joy you bring is immeasurable. Your presence in my life has fueled my determination to complete this book and share its message with the world.

To my mother and father, thank you for instilling in me the values of perseverance, curiosity, and kindness. Your unwavering love and sacrifices have been the cornerstone of my growth and achievements. You have shaped who I am, and for that, I am eternally grateful.

To my brother, your support and belief in me have meant the world. You've always been there to encourage me, challenge me, and remind me of my potential. Your camaraderie has been a source of strength and joy.

I would also like to thank my friends and colleagues who have been my sounding boards, providing invaluable feedback, insights, and motivation when I needed it most. Your constructive criticism and encouragement helped shape this book into something I'm truly proud of.

A special thank you goes to my mentors, teachers, and authors of countless books I have read, whose wisdom and guidance over the years have influenced the philosophies within these pages. You've shown me the power of elimination, not just in theory but through your actions, and for that, I am forever grateful.

Finally, to my readers—thank you for embarking on this journey with me. I hope the lessons and insights in this book inspire you to embrace growth, simplicity, and clarity in your own lives. Your success is my greatest reward.

Foreword

In today's world, we are constantly bombarded with the idea that more is better—more tasks, more goals, more success. We're led to believe that if we just keep adding to our lives, we'll find happiness and fulfillment. But as many of us have discovered, the relentless pursuit of "more" often leaves us overwhelmed, cluttered, and exhausted. Elimination The First Step Towards Growth challenges this mindset with a simple yet profound truth: true growth begins not with addition, but with subtraction.

I was grappling with the same struggles so many of us face—feeling stuck, weighed down by commitments and distractions, and desperately searching for a way forward. Through my personal journey, I discovered that real progress doesn't come from accumulating more, but from letting go of what no longer serves us. This book is the culmination of that realization, and it has been nothing short of transformative.

Elimination The First Step Towards Growth, isn't just another self-help book filled with generic tips and strategies—it's a philosophy, a way of life that encourages you to strip away the unnecessary so you can focus on what truly matters. Within these pages, you'll find practical advice, heartfelt stories, and actionable steps designed to help you reclaim your time, energy, and focus.

Whether you're striving to simplify your work, nurture your relationships, improve your health, or enhance your overall well-being, this book offers a clear roadmap to guide you. The lessons within are rooted in timeless wisdom but are presented in a way that is both relatable and perfectly suited to the complexities of modern life.

I invite you to take this journey with me. As you read, you'll discover that the first step toward genuine growth isn't about doing more but about doing less—removing the clutter, noise, and distractions that have been holding you back. Once you've embraced the power of elimination, you'll find the clarity and space to grow, succeed, and thrive in ways you never imagined possible.

This book has the potential to transform not just your productivity, but your entire outlook on life. It's time to embrace the liberating power of subtraction and start living with purpose and intention.

— Foreword by Rohhan Patil

Preface

Elimination: The First Step Toward Growth in Any Domain

Elimination is the critical foundation for growth in all aspects of life, including money, work, relationships, health, and personal development. Before adding new habits, skills, or relationships that foster growth, one must first remove the negative elements that inhibit progress. By eliminating distractions, toxic behaviors, and unproductive habits, we create space for positive change and intentional improvement.

1. Financial Growth
In the domain of money, eliminating bad spending habits, unnecessary expenses, and debt is the first step toward financial freedom. By reducing impulse buying and curbing lifestyle inflation, individuals can focus on saving, investing, and building wealth. Just as cutting unnecessary financial burdens helps free up resources for investment, eliminating financial clutter provides a clearer path to long-term financial goals.

2. Professional Growth
In the workplace, eliminating inefficiencies such as unproductive tasks, poor time management, or overcommitment paves the way for better performance and career advancement. By streamlining daily tasks and focusing on high-impact activities, professionals can enhance productivity, work smarter, and take on opportunities that lead to personal and professional success.

3. Relationship Growth
Eliminating toxic relationships is essential for emotional well-being and personal growth. Whether it's distancing oneself from harmful individuals or ending draining friendships, removing negative influences opens up space for healthier, more supportive relationships. This, in turn, fosters emotional resilience and stronger connections, enhancing overall life satisfaction.

4. Personal Growth

In personal development, eliminating bad habits such as procrastination, unhealthy eating, or lack of exercise is the first step toward self-improvement. By removing the behaviors that hold us back, we create the conditions needed to build new, positive habits that promote physical health, mental clarity, and emotional balance.

5. Mental Clarity and Focus

Elimination also plays a vital role in managing the mental clutter caused by information overload, digital distractions, and constant multitasking. By cutting out unnecessary information consumption and focusing on mindful engagement, individuals can regain mental clarity and prioritize activities that truly matter. This shift in focus leads to enhanced creativity, better decision-making, and personal fulfillment.

Elimination is the crucial first step toward growth in any domain. It clears the way for intentional progress by removing the obstacles that prevent success. Whether it's finances, work, relationships, or personal well-being, eliminating the negative creates the space needed for positive transformation. Only by shedding the unproductive can we begin to build a more fulfilling, balanced, and successful life.

Prologue

Have you ever felt like no matter how hard you try, the life you want always seems just out of reach? You add more goals, more tasks, more responsibilities, hoping that somehow it will all add up to success—but instead, you're left overwhelmed, stressed, and feeling stuck.

For years, I was caught in that same cycle. I thought growth meant constantly adding things to my life—new habits, more commitments, bigger goals. But the more I added, the more chaotic things became. I was trying to juggle everything, and in the process, I lost sight of what truly mattered. Success seemed further away, not closer.

Then, I discovered something that changed everything: real growth doesn't start by adding; it starts by eliminating. I realized that before we can create the life we want, we have to make space for it. We have to let go of the bad habits, toxic relationships, and unnecessary distractions that weigh us down. Only then can we focus on what truly matters and achieve the extraordinary.

Elimination: The First Step Towards Growth is a guide to help you do just that. This book isn't about quick fixes or adding more to an already overflowing plate. It's about clearing the clutter in your life so you can make room for meaningful growth. It's about understanding that the first step to success is letting go of what no longer serves you.

In the pages that follow, you'll learn how to identify the things holding you back, how to eliminate them, and how to create space for habits and actions that align with your goals. You'll discover that by focusing on less, you can achieve more than you ever thought possible.

This is your invitation to embrace simplicity, clarity, and intentional living. It's time to let go of the chaos and make room for the life you truly deserve. Welcome to the journey of Elimination—the first step toward your extraordinary success.

CHAPTER ONE

INFORMATION OVERLOAD

In the modern age, we live in a world inundated with information. From the moment we wake up, notifications from various social media platforms like WhatsApp, Instagram, and Facebook flood our devices, vying for our attention. This constant bombardment of information leads to a state of cognitive overload, making us feel overwhelmed, anxious, and mentally drained. It's no wonder that managing information has become a central challenge in the pursuit of mental clarity and productivity.

Imagine life just a century ago, not as distant as a thousand years but still relatively different from today. Picture yourself in a small, close-knit village, where people knew each other well and life moved at a measured, natural rhythm. In this setting, information didn't arrive instantly or flood daily routines. News and updates came slowly, typically by word of mouth, passed along during gatherings, or shared over shared tasks. Occasionally, a written letter would arrive, bringing news from distant family members or updates on matters of importance, and such communication took days, even weeks, to reach its destination.

In this quieter era, information was precious and limited, directly relevant to the community's needs and growth. People used the knowledge they gained for practical, meaningful purposes, focusing on skills, relationships, and work that benefited the family and community.

Importance of Information

Information is the cornerstone of knowledge, decision-making, and progress, empowering individuals and societies to solve problems, innovate, and grow. It enables informed choices, mitigates risks, and fosters communication and collaboration, enhancing understanding and connection across communities and borders. In a rapidly changing world, accurate and timely information is critical for navigating challenges, driving innovation, and gaining a competitive edge. Moreover, it preserves cultural and historical heritage, ensuring that the wisdom of the past informs the future. Without reliable information, progress stalls, misunderstandings multiply, and growth opportunities are lost, making it an invaluable resource in every aspect of life.

Information is a powerful tool for making money faster, as it enables individuals and businesses to identify opportunities, optimize investments, and make informed decisions with speed and precision. Access to real-time data and market trends allows for better timing in trading and investing, while insights into consumer behavior and industry dynamics provide a competitive edge in business. Leveraging technology and analytics, driven by information, helps automate processes and uncover profitable patterns, accelerating financial growth. Staying informed about economic policies, emerging markets, and potential risks ensures adaptability and protects against losses. Ultimately, high-quality information empowers smarter strategies, faster scaling, and the ability to seize lucrative opportunities ahead of competitors.

Therefore, throughout human history, the quest to generate, store, and share information has been a defining trait of our species. In the Stone Age, humans carved symbols on rocks and painted cave walls with depictions of animals they hunted. These primitive yet profound methods reflect humanity's early desire to document their experiences and pass on knowledge. As time progressed, the hunger for gathering and preserving information only grew stronger. In the modern world, we generate and store an enormous amount of data daily, ensuring that future generations have access to the accumulated wisdom of the past.

Consider the example of our ancestors' efforts to distinguish between edible and poisonous mushrooms. Many of them sacrificed their lives in the process of trial and error, identifying what was safe to consume and what was lethal. Their discoveries were passed down, sparing future generations from repeating the same fatal mistakes. This is the true value of information: to learn from the past and use that knowledge to navigate the future more wisely.

As the saying goes, "History repeats itself." However, by understanding historical consequences through the lens of preserved information, we can avoid repeating the errors our ancestors made. Knowledge, when effectively gathered and shared, becomes a powerful tool for growth, survival, and progress.

Our relentless pursuit of information—be it through carvings on rocks, written manuscripts, or digital archives—underscores the importance of preserving our collective experiences. It ensures that each generation starts from a stronger foundation, equipped to build upon the lessons of the past.

Now, fast-forward to the present. We live in an era where we consume an overwhelming amount of information daily—more than a person from that small village might have encountered in a lifetime. The volume and speed of information have increased exponentially. **But with this abundance comes a catch: not all information is valuable or meaningful.** Much of what we consume is fleeting, irrelevant, or distracting, often pulling us away from the deeper, more personal pursuits that foster true growth and satisfaction.

In contrast to the past, where knowledge was carefully sifted and appreciated, our challenge today is to filter out the noise and focus on what truly matters for our well-being and personal development. You may have experienced a situation where a friend sends you a meme or reel that you've already seen. While it might be funny or relevant to your current situation, the excitement you feel the first time diminishes when you see it again. Despite this, you may still feel obligated to respond to maintain social norms and make your friend feel acknowledged. This seemingly harmless interaction highlights a deeper issue: our brains are constantly processing unnecessary information. While staying connected with friends and family through social media and messaging platforms has its benefits, the endless stream of updates and notifications contributes significantly to mental clutter. This clutter doesn't just affect our ability to focus; it takes a toll on our overall mental well-being.

Each part of our body ages differently based on how much stress and load it endures, and the brain is no exception. Mental clutter—caused by excessive exposure to irrelevant or redundant information—accelerates the brain's aging process. It leaves us feeling sluggish, fatigued, and less capable of tackling meaningful tasks. In today's digital age, many of us feel perpetually exhausted despite engaging in minimal physical labor. The culprit is often information overload. Every piece of data we consume—be it a meme, a news update, or a viral reel—requires mental energy to process. The more unnecessary information we expose ourselves to, the more strain we place on our brains, leading to mental fatigue that manifests as lethargy throughout the day. By acknowledging and addressing this cycle of overconsumption, we can begin to protect our mental energy, prioritize meaningful interactions, and ultimately lead a more focused and energized.

The solution can only be truly effective when you fully understand the problem in detail. Therefore, let's resist the urge to quickly jump to solutions after reading just one paragraph of this book. Instead, let's take the time to explore the various problem statements surrounding the modern-day clutter. The challenges we face today are diverse and highly personal. For one person, the issue might be an addiction to watching motivational videos; for another, it could be binge-scrolling through Instagram; while someone else might spend entire days glued to sports broadcasts. Each of these situations is unique, and the solutions will vary slightly based on the individual and their habits.

However, there is one universal approach that can work wonders across all these scenarios—a concept that forms the core theme of this book: **Elimination.** It is the first and most crucial step toward growth. By removing unnecessary distractions and habits, we create the space needed for clarity, focus, and meaningful progress.

The "Idiot Box" Transformed

Television, once mockingly referred to as the "Idiot Box," has evolved into one of the most versatile devices of the modern age. From its humble black-and-white beginnings to today's ultra-high-definition smart TVs, it offers endless entertainment options. However, the real question isn't whether television is a technological marvel—it undoubtedly is—but how it impacts our time and productivity, especially when consumed without boundaries.

Many people watch **TV not just for entertainment but also to gain social validation**. For instance, sports enthusiasts often feel compelled to watch every game so they can participate in conversations the next day. Yet, watching an entire game isn't always necessary when quick highlights are readily available. This social pressure to stay updated often leads to excessive screen time, taking away opportunities for more fulfilling or productive activities.

Television and other digital media are undoubtedly entertaining, but they often pull us into passive consumption. Instead of engaging with our own lives, we become immersed in someone else's story on the screen, leaving our narratives untold. Take the example of YouTube influencers who share daily VLOGs of their lives. We find ourselves hooked, watching their routines instead of addressing our own challenges. This phenomenon isn't new—television once did the same through daily soap operas. These shows portrayed the lavish lifestyles of wealthy families, focusing on exaggerated and often illogical problems that most viewers would never encounter in real life.

The logic behind these shows is simple: they are designed to engage your emotional brain. Once they tap into your emotions, they create a temporary sense of pleasure, distracting you from your own harsh realities. These stories comfort us by making us feel that even those with wealth and power have significant problems, diverting attention from solving our own issues. Unfortunately, this form of **escapism** is one of the least productive ways to spend our time. With streaming platforms now more accessible than ever, the temptation has only grown.

Is TV Really That Bad?

Wasn't television one of the greatest inventions of its time? Doesn't it help us reach millions, spread knowledge, and entertain? Or is it just a massive waste of time?

The answers to these questions vary from person to person. Over the years, a common response has been, "It depends on how you use the technology." Isn't that true?

But what if I told you that no matter how you use it—whether for entertainment or knowledge—television can still be harmful? The key issue isn't the content itself but the overuse. If you spend your entire day binge-watching, regardless of whether it's a documentary or a movie, it's bound to have a detrimental impact.

This brings us to the central concept discussed in this book: elimination. When escaping a trap seems impossible, the most effective solution is to remove it altogether. By focusing your energy on eliminating the most time-wasting activities in your life—whether excessive television watching or endless scrolling through social media—you create space for more meaningful pursuits.

However, the thought of eliminating such distractions often fills us with apprehension. What will we do with the vacuum it leaves behind? This void can lead to boredom, a state that many people in today's world dread. With so many entertainment options at our fingertips, boredom feels almost unnatural. Why choose idleness when instant gratification is just a click away? Yet, as uncomfortable as boredom may seem, it holds immense potential for creativity and growth—a theme we'll explore further in the chapters ahead.

Importance of boredom

Boredom, often dismissed as an unpleasant and unproductive state, holds a surprisingly vital role in our lives. In today's fast-paced world, we have multiple options to get entertained throughout the day. we have various devices at our disposal to get hooked up to. However, the natural occurrence of boredom has become increasingly rare, yet its importance cannot be overstated. Here's why boredom is not just beneficial but essential for a well-rounded and creative life:

A Gateway to Creativity

Boredom creates a mental vacuum—a space free from distractions—that can be a powerful catalyst for creativity. When the mind is not preoccupied with external stimuli, it naturally begins to wander, making connections between seemingly unrelated thoughts and ideas. This wandering state often sparks innovative ideas and solutions to problems. Many great artists, inventors, and thinkers have credited their breakthroughs to moments of idleness when their minds were free to explore uncharted territory.

Have you ever found yourself sitting by a flowing river in the evening, doing nothing but observing the gentle movement of the water? Initially, you may feel bored watching the same unchanging flow, but over time, something remarkable happens. Your thoughts and emotions begin to surface, unfolding like pages of a book. This state of mental stillness allows your inner self—the most creative part of your mind—to emerge. After returning home you might have noticed a surge in your willpower.

The next time boredom strikes, resist the urge to grab your phone or seek instant distraction. Instead, take a walk in nature, sit quietly, or simply observe your surroundings. You may be surprised by the clarity, creativity, and inspiration that arise from embracing boredom. It's in these quiet moments that the mind finds space to innovate and the soul reconnects with its essence.

Encourages Self-Reflection

In the absence of external distractions, boredom nudges us to turn inward. It provides an opportunity for introspection, allowing us to assess our feelings, thoughts, and goals. This self-reflection is crucial for personal growth and helps us make more intentional choices about how we live our lives.

Builds Resilience and Patience

Learning to sit with boredom teaches us patience and the ability to tolerate discomfort. In a world where instant gratification is the norm, developing this skill is invaluable. Resilience born from enduring boredom helps us navigate challenges in life with greater composure and strength.

Promotes Problem-Solving Skills

Boredom often arises when our usual ways of engagement no longer satisfy us. This discomfort pushes us to seek new ways to occupy our time, solve problems, or create meaning in our lives. This process fosters innovation and the development of practical skills that might not have emerged in a fully occupied or entertained state.

Restores Mental Energy

Contrary to the constant pursuit of productivity, boredom offers a chance for mental rest. When we step away from overstimulation, our brains have time to recharge, process information, and consolidate memories. This downtime is essential for maintaining mental clarity and long-term productivity.

Strengthens Emotional Well-Being

Boredom allows us to sit with ourselves and confront emotions we might otherwise suppress through constant distraction. This confrontation can lead to greater emotional intelligence, as we learn to understand and manage our feelings rather than escape from them.

Reinforces the Value of Meaningful Activities

Experiencing boredom highlights the difference between mindless distractions and activities that genuinely engage and fulfil us. It helps us appreciate the value of meaningful work, hobbies, and relationships, guiding us toward a more purposeful and satisfying life.

A Catalyst for Exploration

When boredom sets in, it often signals that it's time to explore something new. Whether it's picking up a new hobby, learning a skill, or venturing into unfamiliar territory, boredom pushes us out of our comfort zones and into experiences that can enrich our lives.

Rather than avoiding boredom, we should learn to embrace it as a natural and necessary part of life. By allowing ourselves moments of stillness and inactivity, we create opportunities for growth, creativity, and a deeper understanding of ourselves. In a society that glorifies busyness, boredom reminds us of the beauty and potential of simply being.

Now let us understand the boredom through a story of World War II veterans

The Thrill of Battle and the Quiet of Life

The year was 1944. Amid the chaos of World War II, two soldiers, Jack and Wilhelm, found themselves on opposing sides of a brutal conflict. Jack, an American paratrooper, and Wilhelm, a German infantryman, were strangers bound by fate to meet on the battlefield in Normandy. As bullets flew and the earth trembled, they each fought for survival, their lives teetering on the edge with every passing moment. Yet, amidst the violence, something remarkable happened. Caught in an isolated skirmish, their units obliterated, the two men faced each other in a small clearing. Instead of firing their weapons, they hesitated. In that fleeting moment, they saw not enemies, but two human beings fighting battles beyond the war itself. They lowered their guns and retreated, unknowingly sparing each other's lives.

Fast forward 20 years to 1964. Jack and Wilhelm, now middle-aged men, met again at a veteran's honoring function in Paris. Neither knew the other would be there, but fate, once again, brought them together. As they exchanged pleasantries, Jack suddenly recognized Wilhelm's face. The realization struck both of them like a lightning bolt. They had shared that moment in the clearing, the moment that allowed them to live on to this very day.

Over drinks and shared stories, they recounted their harrowing war days. Jack spoke of the adrenaline that surged through his veins as he parachuted behind enemy lines, every second a gamble with death. Wilhelm recalled the camaraderie of his unit and the quiet terror that accompanied each mission. They laughed, cried, and honoured the lives they had taken and spared. But as their conversation deepened, a shared sentiment emerged.

"Do you ever feel," Jack asked, swirling his glass, "that life... just isn't the same anymore? Like nothing matches the intensity of those days?"

Wilhelm nodded solemnly. "Yes. Life after the war feels... dull. We lived on the edge, Jack. Every moment mattered. Now? It's as if the world is muted."

They both sat in silence, the weight of their words sinking in. War, despite its horrors, had given their lives an unparalleled intensity. Every decision had been life or death, and every sunrise had been a gift. Now, in the calm of peace, they felt adrift, unable to replicate that sense of purpose or exhilaration.

Their discussion soon turned reflective. "I think," Wilhelm ventured, "we raised the bar too high. After feeling so alive in those moments of danger, how can ordinary life ever compare?"

Jack nodded. "It's like we're chasing shadows of that intensity, but it's never the same. And it's not just us. Everyone seems to be chasing something now."

The Post-Pandemic Parallel

This sentiment echoes in our modern world, particularly in the years following the COVID-19 pandemic. The pandemic brought fear, uncertainty, and change—a period where every action felt significant. People lived with heightened awareness, their lives upended in ways they couldn't have imagined. But as the world transitioned back to normal, many found themselves grappling with an unexpected side effect: boredom.

The daily grind, once a source of stability, now feels monotonous. The thrill of adapting to new challenges, whether it was navigating remote work, rediscovering hobbies, or even the simple act of surviving, has faded. People find themselves yearning for excitement, something to reignite that spark of purpose and urgency they felt during the crisis.

This phenomenon, both for the soldiers and for us, stems from the same principle: once the bar of intensity and satisfaction is raised, it's hard to return to baseline. The war provided Jack and Wilhelm with purpose, camaraderie, and adrenaline. The pandemic, though different, created a heightened sense of focus and adaptation for many of us. In both cases, the return to normalcy feels like a step-down.

Reframing the Boredom

Jack and Wilhelm concluded their conversation with a powerful insight. "Perhaps," Jack said, "it's not about trying to replicate those thrills. Maybe it's about finding meaning in the quiet."

Wilhelm smiled. "Yes. The peace we have now? It's something we fought for. It may not be thrilling, but it's valuable."

For us, the lesson is similar. The boredom we feel post-pandemic isn't a sign that life has lost its meaning. Rather, it's an opportunity to rediscover joy in the simple, quiet moments: the laughter of loved ones, the satisfaction of a day's work, or the beauty of an ordinary sunrise. Thrills may be fleeting, but purpose and fulfillment can be cultivated in even the smallest of moments.

Just as Jack and Wilhelm learned to appreciate peace after war, we too must embrace the stability and calm that follow life's storms. Because sometimes, the greatest adventure lies not in chasing thrills, but in learning to cherish the life we've built.

How to Start Eliminating

Consider a familiar scenario: before important exams, many parents cut off cable connections to prevent distractions, ensuring their children focus on studying. What's really happening here is the removal of a major time-consuming activity, creating space for more critical tasks. This approach works because mental energy is limited; if trivial distractions drain it, little remains for meaningful pursuits (more on this in Chapter 2).

If your parents ever did this for you, take a moment to thank them after reading this chapter. They were teaching you a valuable life lesson: eliminating distractions helps you focus on what truly matters.

The same principle can be applied to life's challenges. When the stakes are high, when you feel stuck, or when life becomes overwhelming, ask yourself: **What am I willing to sacrifice in order to grow?**

The answer may surprise you, and it might feel uncomfortable at first. But trust the process—it's worth it. By stepping back and letting go of time-wasting habits or distractions, you create space for new growth. It's like pulling back a slingshot: the temporary retreat allows you to launch forward with greater force.

Identifying and eliminating what's holding you back—be it excessive television, social media, or other unproductive habits—can lead to profound changes in your life. This isn't about mediocrity; it's about preparing yourself to overcome barriers and focus on your true potential. Letting go of these distractions will pave the way for a clearer, more fulfilling journey ahead.

In this section, we'll explore effective techniques to declutter your daily routine, accompanied by stories of individuals who successfully embraced these methods.

Shifting from Passive Consumption to Active Engagement

The first step to overcoming information overload is learning to set boundaries. Passive activities like watching television or scrolling through social media often consume a significant portion of our day without adding much value. Reducing these activities is key to regaining control over your time and energy. Instead of passively consuming content, shift your focus to activities that actively engage your mind and body.

Engage in pursuits that challenge you, bring you joy, or contribute to your personal growth. These might include learning a new skill, dedicating time to exercise, exploring creative hobbies, or simply connecting with loved ones. Such activities provide lasting enrichment compared to the fleeting satisfaction of consuming endless content.

Practicing mindful consumption is another vital aspect of this transformation. Before watching a show or diving into your social media feed, pause and ask yourself: Does this align with my goals or values? If the answer is no, choose to invest your time in something more meaningful. Curating the content you consume allows you to safeguard your mental energy, enhance your emotional well-being, and reclaim control over your daily life.

Breaking the Habit of Information Overload

Bad habits, such as mindlessly scrolling through social media or binge-watching television, contribute significantly to information overload. These behaviours not only drain your mental energy but also trap you in a cycle of passive consumption, leaving little room for productivity or growth. Eliminating such habits is crucial to breaking free from this loop.

Start by setting clear boundaries for your screen time. For example, designate specific times of the day or week for watching television or using social media. Be intentional about the content you engage with—prioritize quality over quantity. By eliminating unnecessary distractions, you create more space in your day for meaningful activities that truly matter.

An effective way to break free is by replacing bad habits with healthier alternatives. For instance, instead of reaching for your phone first thing in the morning, try journaling, meditating, or planning your day. Small, deliberate changes can make a significant difference in the long run.

Remember, breaking free from these patterns isn't just about managing your time—it's about reclaiming your life. Eliminating unproductive habits fosters a shift from passive consumption to active engagement. It allows you to invest your time in personal growth, meaningful relationships, and activities that bring genuine fulfillment.

The Story of Robin: Trapped by the Need to Stay Relevant

Robin had always been an avid sports fan like most of teenage boys. Every weekend, he spent hours glued to the TV, watching football games, basketball matches, and whatever other sport was in season. But his passion for watching sports wasn't just about enjoying the game—it was about staying relevant in his social circle. Every Monday morning, Robin's friends and coworkers gathered around the break room to discuss the weekend's big games. The group always dissected the plays, celebrated the best moments, and debated which team had the best shot at the playoffs. Over time, Robin began to feel an unspoken pressure to keep up. If he missed a game, he felt out of the loop and had little to contribute to the conversation.

At first, it seemed harmless—just part of being part of the "sports tribe." But eventually, it became exhausting. He started sacrificing his weekends, staying up late to watch matches that didn't even interest him, just so he could avoid feeling left out at work. His family noticed that even during dinners or outings, his mind would drift to the TV, anxiously thinking about the game he might miss.

One weekend, while watching a game he didn't particularly care about, Robin realized something: he was spending hours of his life watching sports not out of enjoyment, but out of obligation. Worse, he wasn't using this time for things he truly loved, like spending quality time with his kids or pursuing hobbies that had fallen by the wayside.

That Monday, Robin caught up on highlights in just 15 minutes instead of watching the game. When his friends gathered around to talk about the game, he chimed in briefly with a few key moments and then excused himself. He realized that he didn't need to watch every second of every game to be part of the conversation. Instead, he spent his time more wisely—enjoying life rather than just observing it on a screen.

Over time, Robin found balance. He still loved sports, but now he watched games that genuinely interested him. For everything else, he stuck to quick highlights and spent his reclaimed hours on more fulfilling activities. He realized that social validation wasn't worth sacrificing his own time and happiness.

This is the story of countless teenage boys—and even many adults—who spend a significant portion of their time watching and discussing sports. While sports can be a source of entertainment, community, and inspiration, overindulging in them often yields diminishing returns, especially when the consumption isn't aligned with personal or professional growth.

There's no denying that sports enthusiasts derive joy and a sense of belonging from following their favourite teams and players. However, the hard truth is that only a small fraction of individuals—those whose careers are directly tied to sports, such as athletes, commentators, or analysts—truly benefit professionally from their extensive sports knowledge. For the average 9-to-5 office worker, spending countless hours collecting and analyzing sports statistics or rehashing match details is unlikely to contribute to career advancement or personal development.

Having sports as a hobby is a healthy and recommended outlet, particularly when it involves physical activity. Playing sports enhances fitness, teamwork, and discipline. However, passively consuming sports for hours daily, merely to stay relevant in social discussions, is counterproductive. It siphons precious time that could otherwise be invested in developing new skills, pursuing passions, or achieving long-term goals.

Reassessing Your Social Circles

If your social circle encourages excessive time spent on irrelevant activities like endlessly debating sports matches, it might be time to reevaluate your relationships. Surrounding yourself with individuals who inspire and challenge you to grow is crucial for self-improvement. While engaging in lighthearted sports talk is fine, constantly prioritizing it over meaningful pursuits can stifle your potential.

Consider this perspective: you might have heard of the "10,000-hour rule," which suggests that mastery in any field requires 10,000 hours of deliberate practice. Applying this principle to sports, imagine spending 10,000 hours watching football. Will it make you the next Cristiano Ronaldo? Clearly not. However, dedicating 10,000 hours to actively playing and refining your skills could indeed transform you into a proficient footballer.

The Opportunity Cost

Every hour spent passively consuming sports—or any other form of entertainment—comes at the cost of time that could be invested in personal growth. Time is your most valuable asset, and how you spend it determines the trajectory of your life.

Instead of simply watching others achieve greatness on the field, consider how you could channel that time into something constructive. Whether it's building a new skill, exercising, or working on a passion project, active engagement always yields greater rewards than passive consumption.

A Balanced Approach

Enjoying sports doesn't mean you have to abandon it entirely. The key is moderation and intentionality. Watching an occasional game or following your favourite team is perfectly fine, as long as it doesn't interfere with your priorities or consume disproportionate amounts of time. The goal is to strike a balance that allows you to enjoy sports while still focusing on activities that align with your goals and values.

Final Thought

Life is about making conscious choices that reflect your aspirations and values. While sports can inspire and entertain, let them be a complement to your life, not a distraction from it. Prioritize active participation—both on and off the field—over passive observation. By doing so, you'll not only make better use of your time but also uncover your true potential.

Let's find out some important strategies for managing the daily clutter now.

Strategies for Managing Daily Clutter

Set Boundaries for Information Consumption: Establish specific times for checking emails and social media, and avoid engaging with these platforms outside of designated periods. This helps reduce the constant influx of information and allows you to focus on more meaningful activities.

Curate Your Sources: Be selective about the sources of information you engage with. Subscribe only to those that provide valuable and relevant content. Unfollow or mute sources that contribute to unnecessary clutter.

Practice Mindful Consumption: Approach information consumption with intention. Ask yourself whether the content you are engaging with aligns with your goals and values. If not, consider redirecting your focus.

Embrace Information Detox: Regularly take breaks from information-heavy activities. This could involve digital detoxes or periods of reduced screen time, which will allow your brain to rest and process information more effectively.

Implement a Learning Strategy: Focus on quality over quantity in your learning endeavours. Break down information into manageable chunks, summarize key takeaways, and actively seek ways to apply what you have learned in real-life situations.

Reflect and Adjust: Regularly assess how well you are managing information and its impact on your life. Make adjustments as needed to ensure that your approach to information consumption supports your overall well-being and goals.

By incorporating these strategies, you can better manage the daily clutter of information and create a more balanced and productive lifestyle. Let's see how

A Story of Selective Consumption

Emma was a journalist who thrived on staying informed. Every day, she would open her phone and browse through an endless stream of news articles, blog posts, social media updates, and emails. It seemed like the more she knew, the more effective she would be at her job. Yet, over time, she noticed something unsettling—her focus was deteriorating. Every morning started the same way: Emma would open her phone and be greeted by a flood of notifications. News outlets, social media posts, and email subscriptions poured in, each demanding her attention. She would scroll mindlessly through various social media platforms, catching up on the latest trends and opinions. By the time she sat down to work, her mind was already scattered, filled with a swirl of random, often irrelevant information. Her mornings, instead of being productive, were hijacked by the never-ending flow of data.

As days turned into weeks, Emma began to feel increasingly overwhelmed. Despite spending hours consuming content, she struggled to retain useful information. She noticed that a lot of what she was reading wasn't actually contributing to her personal or professional growth. It was just noise—endless articles that didn't add value, social media posts that cluttered her mind, and notifications that broke her focus. She felt more distracted and less informed than ever before. One afternoon, Emma attended a conference where a speaker discussed the importance of curating information sources. The speaker shared how, in an age of information overload, not all data is created equal. "It's not about how much information you consume," he said, "but about the quality of that information." He talked about how successful people carefully curate the sources they rely on, consuming only what aligns with their goals and values.

The idea struck a chord with Emma. She realized that her problem wasn't just the volume of information but the fact that much of it wasn't useful or relevant. She was giving her time and attention to sources that didn't deserve it. Motivated to make a change, Emma decided to do a complete overhaul of her information consumption habits. That evening, she sat down with her phone and started the process of curation. She unsubscribed from newsletters that didn't provide value and unfollowed social media accounts that didn't contribute to her well-being or professional development. She kept only the news sources that she trusted and that provided in-depth, well-researched articles on topics that mattered to her. Emma also installed a news aggregator app, allowing her to filter articles based on topics relevant to her field, so she could get the best content without wading through irrelevant stories. Social media was another area that needed a cleanup. Emma unfollowed accounts that posted endless memes, trivial updates, or clickbait articles. Instead, she chose to follow accounts that inspired her and shared insights related to her work. She muted some notifications entirely, leaving only the important ones.

Gradually, her newsfeed transformed from a chaotic mess of noise to a streamlined source of quality information.

Emma's next step was to create a routine. Rather than checking her phone throughout the day, she set specific times for catching up on news and social media updates. Every morning, she spent 30 minutes reading the most relevant stories from her trusted sources, then put her phone away to focus on work. In the evening, she allowed herself a brief scroll through social media, but only after her tasks for the day were complete. Within a week, Emma began to notice a difference. Her mornings were more productive. Instead of feeling mentally drained before her day even began, she felt focused and clear-headed. The stories she read were not just informative but also thought-provoking, and they gave her deeper insights that she could apply to her writing. She was no longer bogged down by superficial content or irrelevant distractions. At work, her improved focus translated into better performance. Her articles were more insightful, her deadlines were easier to meet, and she felt more in control of her workload. Outside of work, she found herself less stressed and more present in her personal life. Without the constant barrage of irrelevant updates, her mind felt lighter, and more at ease.

Emma's journey of curating her sources taught her a valuable lesson: when you're selective about the information you consume, you not only save time but also elevate the quality of your thinking. By filtering out the unnecessary, she created mental space for what truly mattered—ideas that could inspire and improve her work and life. In today's world of information overload, Emma learned that being discerning is key. It's not about consuming more but consuming better. By curating your sources, you make room for valuable content that can enrich your life and work, while eliminating the distractions that clutter your mind.

We have reached the conclusion of the first chapter, which underscores a fundamental yet often overlooked truth: eliminating everyday clutter is essential to reclaim the most valuable commodity in a lifetime. Time is the currency of our existence, and how we choose to spend it shapes the quality of our lives.

The first step toward a fulfilling life begins with consciously creating space—both physically and mentally—for what truly matters. The more time you have to focus on your goals, passions, and relationships, the closer you come to living a life of purpose and contentment. Imagine a day when your actions align with your deepest priorities; that is the day when fulfilment begins. We will delve deeper into this transformative concept in Chapter Six, where we explore strategies for optimizing your time to lead a meaningful life.

A Glimpse of What Lies Ahead

In the next chapter, we'll shift our focus to an even more critical aspect of life—your health. The old adage, "health is wealth," carries wisdom that cannot be overstated. Without good health, all the time and resources in the world lose their value. Elimination doesn't just free up time; it also plays a pivotal role in enhancing your physical and mental well-being. By decluttering your life, you create room for healthier habits, reduce stress, and foster a lifestyle that prioritizes vitality over excess.

Stay tuned as we explore how the simple act of letting go can work wonders for your health, ultimately laying the foundation for a life that is not just productive but also profoundly enriching.

CHAPTER TWO

Food & Fitness

Life, for many of us, feels like a constant struggle against a whirlwind of habits and routines. Every day, we set ambitious goals, hoping to break free from the patterns that keep us trapped. But more often than not, we find ourselves back where we started, stuck in a cycle of poor food choices, lack of exercise, and unfulfilled resolutions. In the ancient Indian epic Mahabharata, Lord Krishna teaches Abhimanyu how to enter the Chakravyuha—a complex military formation—but never explains how to escape it. Similarly, many of us are caught in a modern-day Chakravyuha, surrounded by routines and choices that seem impossible to break free from.

w

Every morning, we wake up with the intention of living a productive day. We might tell ourselves that today will be different: we'll start with exercise, eat nutritious food, and avoid distractions. But by the time the day is over, many of us realize we've done the opposite. We skipped the workout, grabbed junk food, and lost ourselves on social media or television. This is the essence of the vicious cycle—one that becomes harder to escape the more we struggle against it.

Motivation may come in bursts, and on some days, we feel invincible. We might exercise, eat well, and check off all the items on our to-do list. But eventually, our energy and willpower fade. As much as we aspire to break free, our habits pull us back in, trapping us in a loop of inconsistency.

The Science of Willpower

The science of willpower reveals that our ability to exercise self-control is not unlimited but rather functions like a muscle that tires with overuse. Every decision we make, whether resisting temptation, solving problems, or maintaining focus, depletes our willpower reserves. This phenomenon, often referred to as "ego depletion," explains why maintaining healthy habits can feel increasingly difficult as the day progresses. For example, while it might be easier to choose a healthy meal in the morning, by evening, after a day of decisions and challenges, the temptation to indulge in less healthy options becomes harder to resist. Willpower also draws from the same pool of mental resources we use for managing stress and emotions, meaning that high stress or emotional upheaval can further drain our capacity for self-control. Understanding this limitation can help us structure our lives to conserve willpower, such as by creating routines, reducing decision fatigue, and using strategies like habit stacking to make healthy behaviors more automatic and less reliant on moment-to-moment self-discipline.

Junk food companies understand this better than anyone. They capitalize on our weakened willpower by bombarding us with advertisements and discounts at the exact times we are most vulnerable—after a long, exhausting day. When you scroll through a food delivery app after work, the brightly colored images of pizzas and burgers are intentionally designed to lure you in. Healthier options, on the other hand, are often more expensive and presented with less visual appeal. This combination of visual cues and pricing strategies can easily derail even the strongest of intentions.

The Exercise-Food Feedback Loop

It's not uncommon for people to think they can offset poor eating habits with exercise. The mentality of "I can eat this junk food because I'll burn it off at the gym" is pervasive. While it's true that occasional indulgences won't necessarily ruin your health, relying on this mindset can lead to inconsistent fitness routines. The truth is, that your gut has a direct connection to your mood. The food you eat influences how you feel, both physically and mentally. When you consume a diet full of processed or junk food, your body becomes sluggish, and your mood often takes a hit. On days when you feel good, you're more likely to engage in physical activity. But if your diet makes you feel lethargic or irritable, the thought of working out can seem impossible. It becomes a self-perpetuating loop: poor food choices lead to low energy, which leads to skipped workouts, which reinforces unhealthy eating habits.

Preparing for Long-Term Success: Diet Before Gym

Every year, millions of people around the world make a New Year's resolution to get fit. January 1st brings a surge in gym memberships, but by February, many of those enthusiastic beginners have already quit. One of the main reasons for this is that they focus on exercise without addressing the more fundamental issue: their diet.

If you want to succeed in adopting a fitness routine, it's crucial to start by correcting your eating habits. Instead of waiting until January to begin your fitness journey, spend December cleaning up your diet. By eliminating junk food and focusing on whole, nutritious meals, you'll start to feel better even before you step foot in the gym. Once your body is fueled by proper nutrition, you'll have more energy, a better mood, and a stronger mindset to tackle your workouts. In doing so, you're setting yourself up for long-term success rather than becoming another statistic of those who quit after the first month.

Understanding the food we consume is important in a day to life and what kind of food will give us the best results in a day to day life certainly helps us feel good throughout the day. In Indian philosophy, particularly Ayurveda and the Bhagavad Gita, food is categorized into three types based on the three gunas or qualities: Sattva (purity), Rajas (activity), and Tamas (inertia). Each type of food influences the body, mind, and soul differently, shaping our energy, emotions, and spiritual tendencies.

1. Sattvik Food (Pure and Harmonious)

Sattvik food is considered the purest type, promoting clarity, calmness, and spiritual growth. It is fresh, natural, and prepared with love and care, focusing on simplicity and nourishment. These foods are easy to digest and enhance vitality, mental clarity, and positivity. Examples include fresh fruits, vegetables, whole grains, nuts, seeds, legumes, milk, and herbal teas. Spices like turmeric, cumin, and coriander are used in moderation. A sattvik diet avoids overly processed, stale, or artificial foods and is associated with a balanced, peaceful lifestyle.

Effects on the body and mind:

- Promotes physical health and energy.
- Cultivates mental clarity, focus, and serenity.
- Encourages compassion and spiritual awareness.

2. Rajsik Food (Stimulating and Energizing)

Rajsik food is associated with passion, ambition, and activity. It fuels the body and mind for action but can sometimes lead to restlessness or hyperactivity if consumed in excess. This category includes foods that are spicy, salty, sour, or rich, such as fried dishes, hot spices, caffeinated beverages, processed snacks, and certain non-vegetarian foods like eggs and meat. While Rajsik foods can be energizing, they are not ideal for those seeking mental peace or spiritual growth, as they can overstimulate the senses and emotions.

Effects on the body and mind:

- Boosts energy and drive for work or competition.
- May lead to restlessness, impatience, or overexcitement.
- Fuels desires and ambitions, often associated with material pursuits.

3. Tamsik Food (Dull and Inertia-Inducing)

Tamsik food is considered heavy, impure, and dull, promoting lethargy and negativity. It includes foods that are stale, overripe, heavily processed, fermented, or prepared with excessive oil, sugar, or preservatives. Examples are alcohol, tobacco, junk food, leftovers, and meat from animals treated inhumanely. Tamsik foods are harder to digest, leading to sluggishness and clouded judgment. They are thought to increase ignorance, laziness, and a lack of spiritual awareness.

Effects on the body and mind:

- Causes lethargy, heaviness, and a lack of energy.
- Encourages negative emotions like anger, greed, and ignorance.
- It can weaken immunity and lead to physical and mental imbalances.

Practical Applications

Sattvik food is ideal for those seeking a balanced, peaceful lifestyle with a focus on physical and spiritual health.

Rajsik food is suitable for people leading active lives or requiring high energy but should be balanced with sattvik elements.

Tamsik food should be avoided or minimized as it hampers overall well-being and productivity.

Ayurveda emphasizes moderation and **mindful eating**, recognizing that food not only nourishes the body but also shapes our thoughts, emotions, and spiritual journeys.

let's shift our focus now to understand the importance of mindful eating.

The Importance of Mindful Eating

One of the most common mistakes people make with food is not paying attention to what they eat. In today's fast-paced world, meals are often eaten in front of the TV, during work calls, or while scrolling through social media. This mindless consumption disconnects us from our bodies' signals. We don't realize which foods nourish us and which ones leave us feeling bloated, sluggish, or uncomfortable.

Mindful eating, on the other hand, encourages us to slow down and pay attention to our food. It's about savoring every bite, chewing thoroughly, and listening to how our body responds. This practice can help us identify food intolerances, such as lactose or gluten sensitivity, which often go unnoticed because we aren't paying attention to how we feel after eating. In fact, many people continue eating foods that don't agree with them simply because they've been part of their diet for years.

To practice mindful eating, try turning every meal into a ritual. Sit down at the table without distractions—no TV, no phone, no multitasking. Focus entirely on your food. Chew each bite slowly and aim to chew 32 times before swallowing. This simple practice can improve digestion, enhance your relationship with food, and lead to better overall health.

Mindful eating can help us to increase digestion, but it will also not always help if you are constantly consuming Tamsik food. slowly it will deteriorate your digestion and will lead to multiple health issues. therefore it becomes important that we focus on eliminating the Tamsik food completely from our diet.

In recent years, elimination diets have emerged as a powerful tool for individuals seeking to improve their health, identify food intolerances, and enhance overall well-being. At its core, the concept of an elimination diet is simple yet profound: remove potentially problematic foods from your diet for a set period of time, and then gradually reintroduce them, one by one. This systematic approach allows you to determine which foods may be causing issues such as digestive discomfort, skin irritations, or even mood swings.

The Power of Elimination Diets

The process of an elimination diet is methodical and requires patience. Typically, the first phase involves eliminating common allergens and inflammatory foods such as dairy, gluten, soy, eggs, and processed sugars. During this time, you focus on consuming whole, unprocessed foods that are unlikely to cause adverse reactions. This phase usually lasts anywhere from two to six weeks, giving your body time to reset and heal.

After this period, you slowly reintroduce the eliminated foods, one at a time. Each food is consumed for several days while you closely monitor your body's reactions. Are you experiencing bloating, fatigue, skin breakouts, or mood changes? If so, it's possible that the reintroduced food may be problematic for your system. By tracking these reactions, you can identify which foods your body can tolerate and which ones it cannot. This deliberate process of elimination and reintroduction may feel slow, but it is incredibly enlightening. The more carefully you approach it, the clearer the picture becomes about how your body reacts to specific foods. What you discover can be life-changing.

Uncovering Hidden Food Intolerances

One of the most significant benefits of an elimination diet is uncovering hidden food intolerances. Many people suffer from chronic issues like fatigue, brain fog, bloating, or even persistent skin conditions without realizing that the foods they are eating could be the culprits. Often, these symptoms are subtle or slow to appear, making it difficult to connect them directly to specific foods. The elimination diet serves as a powerful tool to isolate and identify these triggers.

For example, someone may unknowingly have a sensitivity to gluten or dairy. Before starting the elimination diet, they might experience frequent headaches, joint pain, or digestive discomfort but never associate these symptoms with their diet. However, once gluten or dairy is removed, they may notice a remarkable improvement in their symptoms, providing a clear signal that their body does not tolerate these foods well.

This newfound awareness allows individuals to take control of their health. By avoiding foods that trigger negative reactions, they can prevent symptoms from recurring and improve their overall quality of life. For many, this marks the beginning of a journey toward better health, greater energy, and a more balanced mood.

Boosting Energy and Mood

One of the most profound changes that individuals often experience after completing an elimination diet is a significant improvement in energy levels and mood stability. Many people who suffer from fatigue or mood swings don't realize that their diet plays a pivotal role in these conditions.

When you remove foods that don't serve your body, you give your system the opportunity to function optimally.

Improved gut health is often at the heart of these benefits. The gut is sometimes referred to as the "**second brain**" because of its close connection to mental health and emotional well-being. When the gut is inflamed or irritated by foods your body can't tolerate, it can lead to a host of issues, including anxiety, depression, or irritability. By eliminating the foods causing this inflammation, your gut health improves, and as a result, your mood stabilizes. Restoring balance in your digestive system can also have a ripple effect on other areas of your life. With higher energy levels and a more balanced emotional state, you may find it easier to stay motivated and stick to a consistent fitness routine. Exercise no longer feels like a burden, and making healthy choices becomes more natural. The body is no longer fighting against itself; instead, it's working with you, supporting your efforts to lead a healthier, more active lifestyle.

Breaking the Cycle of Poor Eating Habits

For many, an elimination diet represents the first step in breaking the vicious cycle of poor eating habits and inconsistent health routines. When we eat foods that don't agree with our bodies, we often experience cravings for unhealthy options, leading to a downward spiral of poor nutrition. For example, someone with a sensitivity to sugar might find themselves craving more sugary foods, leading to mood swings and energy crashes.

Eliminating these problem foods can stop this cycle in its tracks. Once the body is no longer bombarded by the very foods that cause it harm, cravings for junk food often diminish, and the desire for healthier options increases. Many people report that after completing an elimination diet, they no longer feel the same intense cravings for processed snacks or sugary treats. Instead, they naturally gravitate toward whole, nourishing foods that make them feel good.

This shift is transformative because it's not about willpower alone—it's about fundamentally changing how your body responds to food. By listening to your body's signals and honoring what it needs, you can cultivate a healthier, more sustainable approach to eating.

Long-Term Benefits and Empowerment

Some argue that eliminating certain types of food from the diet may lead to nutritional deficiencies, potentially compromising the immune system and adversely affecting the body. They are not entirely wrong; if the diet is not followed correctly or without the guidance of an expert, it could indeed result in nutritional imbalances. However, most individuals are capable of distinguishing between Sattvik and Tamsik foods. Before consulting a nutritionist, you can begin by gradually eliminating Tamsik foods and observing the changes. The results are often transformative, as removing harmful elements from your life can create remarkable improvements.

The long-term benefits of an elimination diet go far beyond immediate symptom relief. Once you identify the foods that best support your health, you gain the power to make informed choices that enhance your overall well-being. No longer at the mercy of unexplained ailments or uncontrollable cravings, you acquire the knowledge and tools to maintain balance, vitality, and health for a lifetime.

Many who undertake an elimination diet describe it as a transformative journey. Not only do they develop a clearer understanding of how food impacts their bodies, but they also foster a deeper connection to their own health and wellness. This newfound awareness promotes a sense of empowerment that extends to all areas of life, including fitness, mental health, and self-care.

John's Journey: A Personal Transformation

John, a 35-year-old marketing professional, had always struggled with fatigue, poor digestion, and frequent mood swings. Despite his best efforts to maintain a healthy lifestyle, he found himself relying on processed foods, caffeine, and alcohol to get through the day. His daily routine was predictable: a sugary breakfast cereal to start the day, several cups of coffee to stay alert during work, fast food for lunch, and a few beers in the evening to unwind. On weekends, he would often indulge in large meals and enjoy beers with friends, but he felt sluggish and bloated afterward.

John's health started to deteriorate as his energy levels plummeted, and he became more dependent on caffeine and sugar to get through the day. He frequently experienced digestive issues, like bloating and stomach cramps, and he couldn't seem to shake off a persistent feeling of exhaustion. He tried various quick fixes—more coffee, energy drinks, and even crash diets—but nothing worked in the long term.

One day, after a particularly bad bout of indigestion following a weekend of heavy eating and drinking, John decided it was time for a change. He had heard about elimination diets and their potential benefits, so he decided to give it a try. He committed to eliminating processed foods, tea, coffee, and alcohol from his diet for 30 days to see if it would improve his health.

At first, John struggled with the drastic changes. The first few days without his morning coffee left him with headaches and low energy, but he stuck with it. Giving up processed food was equally challenging, as he had to find healthier alternatives and cook meals from scratch. Replacing beer and alcohol with water and herbal teas was tough, especially during social events, but he remained committed to his goal.

By the end of the first week, John noticed something unexpected—his digestion was improving. The constant bloating he had experienced for years began to subside, and he no longer felt the need to rush to the restroom after every meal. By the second week, his energy levels started to rise. He wasn't relying on caffeine to get through the day, and he felt more alert in the afternoons, a time when he would usually hit a wall.

By the third week, John was waking up in the morning feeling refreshed, something he hadn't experienced in years. His mood swings became less frequent, and his overall mental clarity improved. He was more productive at work and found himself less irritable in social situations.

By the end of the 30 days, John had experienced a complete transformation. His skin had cleared up, his digestive issues were gone, and he had more energy than he had in years. But perhaps the most significant change was his mood. Without the spikes and crashes caused by sugar, caffeine, and alcohol, John's emotions stabilized. He felt more in control of his life and his decisions.

With his newfound energy, John started exercising regularly. He no longer dreaded going to the gym, as he had the stamina to complete his workouts. His cravings for junk food and sugary snacks diminished, and he found himself naturally gravitating toward healthier options like fruits, vegetables, and lean proteins.

John also noticed that his social life improved. Instead of meeting friends for drinks, he started suggesting healthier activities like hikes or fitness classes. He found that he could still enjoy socializing without relying on alcohol, and his relationships became more meaningful as a result.

After the 30-day elimination phase, John began to reintroduce some foods to see how his body would react. He started with small amounts of coffee but found that even one cup made him jittery and anxious, so he decided to limit his caffeine intake to occasional green tea. He also tried having a beer but realized it made him feel bloated and sluggish the next day. As a result, he chose to drink alcohol only on rare occasions and stick to water and herbal teas as his primary beverages.

John also realized that processed foods, particularly those high in sugar and artificial ingredients, triggered his digestive issues and mood swings. Instead of returning to his old eating habits, he continued to cook meals from scratch, using whole, unprocessed ingredients.

For John, the elimination diet was more than just a temporary fix—it was a lifestyle change. By identifying the foods that didn't serve him, he was able to take control of his health in a way that no crash diet or quick fix could. His energy levels remained high, his mood stable, and his digestive issues were a thing of the past. The power of elimination diets lies in their ability to help people like John uncover the hidden culprits behind their health issues. By giving up processed food, coffee, tea, and beer, John was able to break free from the cycle of poor eating habits and transform his health for the better. His story is a testament to the profound impact that mindful, deliberate changes can have on one's life.

The Japanese concept of Hara Hachi Bu

which translates to "eat until you're 80% full," is a practice rooted in the island of Okinawa, home to some of the world's longest-living people. This cultural principle is both a dietary guideline and a philosophy of moderation, reflecting a mindful approach to eating that has been linked to improved health and longevity.

At its core, Hara Hachi Bu encourages individuals to stop eating when they feel about 80% full, rather than continuing until they feel completely satiated. The idea is to leave some room in the stomach, avoiding the discomfort and potential health risks associated with overeating. Physiologically, this approach aligns with the **body's natural satiety signals, which can take about 20 minutes to register in the brain** after eating. People practicing Hara Hachi Bu reduce the likelihood of consuming excess calories by eating slowly and stopping before feeling completely full.

The principle is deeply connected to the Okinawan lifestyle, where people consume nutrient-dense, plant-based meals rich in vegetables, tofu, sweet potatoes, and small amounts of fish. Their diet is low in processed foods and sugars, further contributing to their exceptional health outcomes. This moderation in food intake helps maintain a healthy weight, reduces the risk of chronic diseases like diabetes and heart disease, and supports overall metabolic health.

Hara Hachi Bu is not just about portion control but also about cultivating mindfulness and gratitude during meals. By paying attention to hunger and fullness cues, individuals can develop a better relationship with food, savoring each bite and appreciating the nourishment it provides. This practice aligns with broader Japanese cultural values of balance and simplicity, promoting harmony not only in eating habits but also in life.

In modern times, where overeating and obesity have become significant health challenges worldwide, adopting the Hara Hachi Bu principle can be a powerful tool for fostering healthier eating habits. It serves as a reminder that moderation, mindfulness, and respect for the body can pave the way for a longer, healthier, and more fulfilling life.

When you overeat, your body diverts a significant amount of energy and resources toward digestion, often at the expense of other essential bodily functions and mental clarity. The digestive process is energy-intensive, involving the breakdown of food, nutrient absorption, and waste elimination. When the digestive system is constantly overworked due to excessive food intake, it can strain the body and diminish its capacity to focus on other critical aspects of physical and mental well-being.

For instance, instead of allocating energy to repairing cells, strengthening the immune system, or optimizing brain function, the body prioritizes digesting the large quantity of food consumed. This can lead to feelings of lethargy and sluggishness, commonly referred to as a "food coma." With the brain and other systems deprived of sufficient energy, concentration, creativity, and productivity can take a hit.

From a long-term perspective, chronic overeating can result in metabolic imbalances, weight gain, and increased risk of conditions such as diabetes, heart disease, and fatty liver. This not only impacts physical health but also mental health, as conditions like obesity are often associated with lower self-esteem and increased stress or anxiety. Furthermore, an overworked digestive system may eventually become inefficient, leading to problems like indigestion, bloating, or even gastrointestinal disorders.

On the other hand, eating in moderation allows the body to digest food efficiently while leaving energy available for other crucial activities. A balanced diet supports overall health by enabling the body to focus on healing, improving immunity, and enhancing mental sharpness. With fewer distractions caused by heavy digestion, the mind can engage more deeply in creative endeavors, problem-solving, and meaningful interpersonal interactions.

Adopting mindful eating practices, such as consuming smaller, nutrient-dense meals, not only supports digestion but also empowers the individual to prioritize their time and energy on pursuits that enrich their life, rather than being caught in a cycle of overindulgence and recovery, eating moderately can foster a harmonious balance between nourishing the body and fulfilling one's personal, professional, and creative aspirations.

Let's see another story of a person who has severe digestion issues which makes it difficult on focusing day to day activities.

The Story of Mark: Overcoming Years of IBS Struggles

Mark had been dealing with the symptoms of Irritable Bowel Syndrome (IBS) for as long as he could remember. Every day felt like a battle. Stomach cramps, bloating, and unpredictable bowel movements made even simple activities stressful. Going out for dinner with friends, traveling, or even just attending meetings at work was a constant source of anxiety. He tried different diets, over-the-counter medications, and self-diagnosed remedies, but nothing seemed to bring long-lasting relief.

The physical symptoms were bad enough, but the mental and emotional toll was equally exhausting. Mark often found himself skipping social events, afraid of the discomfort or embarrassment his condition might cause. He had grown tired of trying new treatments that only offered temporary solutions. After years of struggle, he felt like he was running out of options, and the frustration was overwhelming.

One day, after hearing about a gastroenterologist with a reputation for treating complex digestive issues, Mark decided to seek professional help. Dr. Jacobs, the specialist, took a very different approach than what Mark had experienced before. Instead of focusing solely on managing the symptoms, Dr. Jacobs was committed to identifying the root causes of Mark's IBS.

After a series of tests, Dr. Jacobs discovered that Mark's condition was being triggered by food intolerances that he had never been fully aware of, including gluten and lactose sensitivity. Additionally, stress was found to be a significant factor in worsening his symptoms. Dr. Jacobs created a comprehensive treatment plan for Mark, which included an elimination diet to identify problematic foods, probiotic supplements, and a focus on stress management techniques like mindfulness and yoga.

The elimination diet was challenging at first, but Mark stuck with it. After a few weeks, he began to notice something incredible—his symptoms were reducing. The bloating was less frequent, the cramps were subsiding, and he no longer felt chained to the nearest restroom. After months of trial and error, Mark found out which foods were triggering his IBS and which ones he could eat without issues.

But it wasn't just about food. Dr. Jacobs also emphasized the importance of managing stress, which Mark hadn't realized was playing such a big role in his condition. By incorporating yoga and meditation into his daily routine, Mark found that his overall well-being improved significantly. His anxiety decreased, and with it, his IBS symptoms became far more manageable.

After years of struggling with IBS, Mark finally felt like himself again. He had energy, he could plan trips without worry, and he began to enjoy social gatherings without the constant fear of discomfort. He realized that finding the right doctor and approach to treatment made all the difference. Dr. Jacobs' holistic method of focusing on diet, stress, and long-term health gave Mark the relief he had been searching for.

Today, Mark continues to manage his IBS, but he feels empowered, healthy, and in control of his life for the first time in years.

Both stories resonate across the globe, as lifestyle changes coupled with poor eating habits continue to take a toll on our health. This is the story of you and me—those who often opt for quick, convenient bites of outside food to satisfy our hunger. However, just as John and Mark were able to reverse their unhealthy habits, so can we by following the steps outlined in their stories. The process involves identifying the problem (Tamsik food habits), eliminating those unhealthy choices, and replacing them with healthier (Sattvik) alternatives.

Since we have taken the first step of eliminating bad food choices, let's now shift our focus to Eliminating the Sedentary lifestyle. Which is crucial for maintaining long-term health and preventing a range of chronic conditions that are increasingly common in today's digital and convenience-driven world. Prolonged inactivity, such as sitting for extended periods, has been linked to higher risks of obesity, heart disease, type 2 diabetes, and even certain types of cancer. Regular physical activity, by contrast, helps regulate weight, improves cardiovascular health, boosts metabolism, and strengthens muscles and bones. Beyond physical health, eliminating sedentary habits also has significant mental health benefits. Sitting for long hours can contribute to feelings of fatigue, stress, and anxiety, while regular movement stimulates the release of endorphins, which promote a positive mood and reduce symptoms of depression. Moving more throughout the day can also enhance focus, productivity, and cognitive function, reducing mental fatigue and improving overall well-being. In addition, increasing physical activity helps improve sleep quality, regulate blood sugar levels, and maintain good posture, which is often compromised by prolonged sitting. Small changes, such as incorporating walking breaks, standing desks, or active hobbies, can make a significant difference, leading to a healthier, more balanced lifestyle.

Importance of Walking

Walking is a powerful and accessible form of exercise that offers a wealth of physical, mental, and emotional benefits. One of its greatest advantages is its simplicity—walking requires no gym membership, special equipment, or prior training, making it easy for anyone to incorporate into their daily routine. Physically, walking is an excellent cardiovascular workout that helps improve circulation, lower blood pressure, and reduce the risk of heart disease and stroke. It also strengthens muscles, particularly in the legs, hips, and lower back, while improving joint flexibility and mobility. For individuals managing weight, walking is an effective way to burn calories and maintain a healthy body weight without putting undue stress on the body.

Mentally, walking has the power to clear the mind and reduce mental fatigue. The rhythmic motion of walking and the release of endorphins (the body's natural "feel-good" hormones) can significantly boost mood and reduce symptoms of depression and anxiety. Studies show that even a short, brisk walk can have immediate effects on reducing stress levels, making it a natural remedy for managing daily pressures. Walking in nature, particularly in green spaces or near water, offers additional benefits, including improved concentration, creativity, and cognitive function. The combination of physical activity and exposure to nature has been shown to lower cortisol levels (the stress hormone) and increase feelings of calm and contentment.

Walking also promotes better sleep by regulating circadian rhythms and encouraging the release of sleep-inducing hormones like melatonin. It offers a low-impact alternative to more intense forms of exercise, making it suitable for individuals of all ages, including those with joint issues or chronic health conditions. Additionally, walking encourages social interaction when done with friends, family, or in walking groups, further enhancing its mental and emotional benefits. Whether it's a leisurely stroll in the park or a brisk walk around the block, walking remains one of the most beneficial, sustainable, and universally accessible activities for improving both physical and mental health.

Walking in nature is an incredibly restorative activity that offers profound benefits for both the body and mind. The natural environment provides a sense of peace and tranquility that can't be replicated by indoor settings, making it a powerful antidote to the stresses of modern life. Studies have shown that spending time outdoors, especially in green spaces, reduces levels of cortisol (the stress hormone), lowers blood pressure, and improves heart health. The sights, sounds, and smells of nature, from rustling leaves to bird songs, create a sensory experience that calms the mind and enhances focus, promoting a state of mindfulness. Furthermore, walking in nature has been linked to improved mood, reduced anxiety, and greater emotional well-being, as exposure to natural settings can foster feelings of awe, connection, and contentment. Nature walks also encourage deeper breathing and help reset the body's internal rhythms, improving sleep patterns and boosting energy. Beyond physical and mental health, walking in nature provides an opportunity for reflection and introspection, offering clarity and helping to cultivate a sense of balance and perspective.

Sport as Exercise

Engaging in sports is not only a great way to stay physically fit, but it also plays a significant role in developing important life skills, mental resilience, and emotional well-being. Regular participation in sports promotes cardiovascular health, muscle strength, and flexibility, helping to reduce the risk of chronic diseases like obesity, diabetes, and heart disease. Beyond the physical benefits, sports foster teamwork, discipline, and time management teaching individuals how to work collaboratively, set goals, and maintain focus under pressure. These skills translate well into personal and professional life, encouraging a balanced, goal-oriented approach. Mentally, sports can reduce stress, improve mood, and enhance cognitive function, as physical activity stimulates the release of endorphins, the body's natural mood boosters. Moreover, sports can teach valuable lessons in resilience and perseverance, helping individuals cope with setbacks and challenges. Whether it's through competition or recreation, sports also provide an avenue for social connection, as they encourage interaction, cooperation, and camaraderie among people from diverse backgrounds. In essence, sports contribute to a holistic sense of well-being, offering benefits that extend far beyond the playing field.

"The secret of success is to come back tomorrow"

In the journey toward fitness, one of the most common mistakes people make is going all out in a single session—lifting heavy weights, running long distances, or doing intense cardio—and then feeling too sore or demotivated to return the next day. While their intentions are admirable, this approach often leads to burnout, injuries, or frustration, halting progress entirely.

The truth is, fitness isn't achieved in a day—it's a result of consistent, steady effort over time. The saying "The secret of success is to come back tomorrow" holds profound relevance in the world of fitness. Here's why:

Fitness is a Marathon, Not a Sprint

Your body needs time to adapt to new challenges. Doing too much in one day doesn't accelerate progress; instead, it overwhelms your muscles and mind. The real progress happens when you engage in manageable workouts day after day. Consistency builds endurance, strength, and resilience far more effectively than sporadic bursts of effort.

Recovery is Part of the Process

Muscles grow and strengthen during recovery, not during the workout itself. If you overdo it on Day 1 and skip Day 2 due to soreness or exhaustion, you're breaking the cycle of consistency. A sustainable approach—where you show up regularly and allow for recovery—ensures long-term progress and minimizes the risk of injury.

Building Habits, Not Just Strength

Fitness success depends on developing habits. Habits form through repetition, not intensity. When you commit to showing up tomorrow—whether it's for a light stretch, a walk, or a short workout—you train your mind and body to make fitness a regular part of your life. Over time, this habit becomes second nature, and the results follow naturally.

Small Steps Add Up

Imagine you aim to climb a mountain. Taking one huge leap won't get you there; it's the small, steady steps that make the journey possible. In fitness, every workout, no matter how small, contributes to your progress. Even if you don't feel like working out, showing up for 10 minutes is better than skipping entirely. Those small efforts compound over time, leading to significant transformation.

Motivation Will Wane; Discipline Will Sustain

There will be days when you don't feel motivated to exercise. But success isn't about how you feel on any single day; it's about your ability to return tomorrow. Discipline—fueled by the mindset of coming back tomorrow—is what turns fitness from a temporary phase into a lasting lifestyle.

Practical Steps to "Come Back Tomorrow"

Start Small: *Instead of a marathon workout, begin with manageable sessions that leave you energized rather than exhausted.*

Focus on Consistency: *Aim for sustainable daily efforts rather than sporadic high-intensity workouts.*

Track Your Progress: *Celebrate small victories to stay motivated.*

Listen to Your Body*: Adjust the intensity to maintain regularity and avoid burnout.*

Commit to Showing Up*: Even on low-energy days, do a light activity to keep the habit alive.*

Fitness is not a one-day event but a lifelong journey. The secret to success lies in your ability to show up consistently, day after day. Whether it's a full workout, a walk, or simply stretching, the act of "coming back tomorrow" ensures steady progress over time.

By embracing this mindset, you'll build a sustainable routine, achieve your fitness goals, and transform your life—one day at a time.

The central theme of this book is the power of elimination—a concept many people fear. We often associate elimination with the feeling of loss, which our human brain instinctively equates with pain. As a species wired for **loss aversion**, we feel more distress when we lose something than joy when we gain something. This fear makes it challenging to let go of habits, things, or even people that no longer serve us. In the next chapter, we will explore the importance of letting go—eliminating toxic people from our lives to foster personal growth and well-being.

CHAPTER THREE

RELATIONSHIP

Relationships form the core of our existence, and from the moment we are born, we are thrust into a web of relationships that shape our experiences and our lives. Our relatives, for instance, are given to us by default, not by choice. Parents, siblings, cousins, uncles, and aunts—these relationships are like building blocks of our social existence, but the way we engage with them is within our control. We can decide how much time and energy we invest in each relationship, choosing to nurture some and avoid others.

But relationships go beyond just relatives. As we grow, we have the power to choose friends, partners, and other significant relationships that can either add value to our lives or detract from our well-being. It's crucial to realise that while some relationships are born from obligation, others are formed out of choice, and managing both requires emotional intelligence, courage, and self-awareness.

The saying that "happiness increases after sharing while sadness decreases" captures a fundamental truth about the human experience: our emotions are deeply interconnected with social interaction and the support of others. When we experience happiness, whether it's the joy of an achievement, a beautiful moment, or a personal victory, sharing this happiness with others often amplifies the positive feelings. The act of sharing allows us to relive the experience, express our joy, and connect with others who may also celebrate with us. This shared experience fosters a sense of community and belonging, strengthening relationships and reinforcing positive emotions. When we talk about our happiness, we invite others into our joy, and their shared excitement or appreciation can make us feel even more fulfilled.

On the other hand, when we are sad or going through a difficult time, sharing our sorrow with others can help reduce the weight of that sadness. The emotional support we receive from friends, family, or even a therapist provides comfort, validation, and understanding. Just as happiness is amplified when shared, sadness is diminished when it is expressed and acknowledged by others. Speaking about our struggles can provide a sense of release, helping to lighten our emotional load. This is often why people feel a sense of relief after opening up about their problems—simply knowing that someone else understands or cares can be incredibly therapeutic.

Moreover, the process of sharing sadness can lead to practical support, whether in the form of advice, assistance, or just a listening ear. This shared vulnerability creates deeper connections with others, fostering empathy and compassion. It also allows us to see that we are not alone in our pain, which can provide a sense of hope and perspective. While happiness naturally grows in the act of sharing, sadness tends to shrink when shared because the burden of the emotion is divided between people, allowing for healing and comfort.

In essence, the dynamic of sharing both happiness and sadness is an essential part of human connection. Our emotions are amplified or lessened by the way we interact with others, making sharing a powerful tool for emotional well-being. Whether it's celebrating the good times or seeking solace in the hard times, sharing our feelings not only strengthens relationships but also enhances our own capacity to cope with the ups and downs of life.

The Role of Karma in Relationships

According to Hindu philosophy, a child's karma begins to activate around the age of three. Before this age, a child is seen as karma-free, existing in a pure, untainted state. At the age of three, the child begins to draw from their store of "sanchit karma," the accumulated karma from previous lives and starts interacting with their environment. The environment, particularly the relationships a child experiences, influences the type of karma they begin to express.

For instance, a nurturing and positive environment can help a child tap into good karma, leading to healthier relationships throughout their life. Conversely, a chaotic or negative environment may lead to the manifestation of negative karma, resulting in toxic relationships and interpersonal struggles. Understanding this connection between karma and relationships is critical to navigating life's social complexities. Every relationship, whether familial or chosen, plays a role in our karmic journey, influencing our spiritual growth and life experiences.

If we take this concept of karma seriously, it becomes evident how our early surroundings and relationships play a significant role in shaping our journey.
his understanding highlights the importance of spending time with people who uplift and encourage personal growth, as opposed to those who stifle or drag us down.

The Power of Choice in Friendships

Unlike our family, we have the freedom to choose our friends. Friendships are often seen as the most voluntary of relationships, making them incredibly important. Good friends can be like gems, offering support, joy, and companionship throughout life. However, choosing the right friends can be challenging. It requires discernment, emotional intelligence, and at times, the courage to let go of friendships that no longer serve us.

It is difficult to sever ties with people, especially when emotions are involved. Yet, it is often necessary to distance oneself from toxic friends who drain your energy, bring negativity, or lead you down unproductive paths. Such relationships can limit your personal growth, keeping you stuck in patterns that don't align with your true goals or values. The courage to cut ties, even if it means moving cities or breaking long-standing bonds, can be a life-changing decision.

Toxic friends can have a deeply negative impact on both your personal growth and emotional well-being. They often create an environment where your progress is stunted, either by discouraging you from pursuing your goals or subtly undermining your efforts. Such individuals tend to have a mindset that resists personal responsibility, blaming external factors for their own shortcomings instead of looking inward. This projection can lead them to criticize or manipulate others, especially those closest to them, in order to deflect attention away from their failures. One of the most harmful behaviours of toxic friends is their ability to make you feel guilty for wanting more out of life—whether it's striving for personal success, seeking new opportunities, or trying to improve your circumstances. They may use emotional manipulation, guilt-tripping, or passive-aggressive tactics to make you feel as though your aspirations are selfish or unjustified, even though pursuing your own happiness and growth is essential for your well-being. Recognizing these destructive patterns is key to breaking free from their influence. Once you can identify how these friends undermine your potential and contribute to your emotional burden, you can start setting boundaries and distancing yourself from the negativity they bring into your life. This self-awareness allows you to reclaim your power and create space for healthier, more supportive relationships that encourage your growth and success.

Toxic Family Dynamics

While friendships can be chosen, family is a different matter altogether. Our relationships with family members, particularly parents, often shape much of our early understanding of love, responsibility, and social norms. However, even family relationships can be toxic. Parents, in particular, may impose their own dreams, desires, and societal expectations onto their children, which can lead to a great deal of pressure and internal conflict.

Parents often have a standard set of expectations for their children: get a good education, secure a stable job, get married, have children, and so on. While these aspirations may be rooted in care and concern, they can often suffocate a child's true potential, especially if the child's natural talents or interests don't align with these conventional paths.

The Bollywood movie 3 Idiots offers a powerful critique of this pressure-filled approach, where parents push their children into predefined roles like doctor or engineer, ignoring their passions. In many Asian cultures, societal success is measured by wealth and status, rather than personal fulfillment or happiness. This creates an environment where children grow up valuing external achievements over personal joy or creativity.

In households with "tiger parents"—(highly demanding and competitive parents)—children often experience immense pressure to excel in every aspect of life. The constant need to perform can lead to burnout, health issues, and a deep sense of inadequacy, even in adulthood. These children often grow up feeling that they must always meet external expectations, leaving little room for self-discovery or emotional growth.

Breaking Away from Parental Expectations

While the influence of family, particularly parents, is significant, it is possible—and often necessary—to break free from their expectations. In many Western cultures, children leave home for college or work early, which allows them to establish independence and explore life on their own terms. In contrast, in Asian families, children often stay with their parents until they marry, which can prolong dependency and inhibit personal growth.

Living independently, even for a short time, can be incredibly liberating. It allows you to carve out your own identity, free from the immediate influence of family expectations. This space for self-exploration can lead to stronger, more meaningful relationships with your family, as well. When you return home after being away, the relationship dynamic shifts, and mutual respect is more likely to grow. Absence makes the heart grow fonder, and your value in the eyes of your parents may increase as they see you as a capable, self-reliant adult.

Most Asian parents care deeply for their children and, as a result, often don't encourage them to gain full independence until they are married. While this comes from a place of love and concern, it can inadvertently lead to children becoming overly dependent on their families, especially their parents. Living with family and being independent each comes with its own set of advantages and challenges. However, one crucial lesson in life is that time doesn't wait for anyone, and sooner or later, you must take charge of your own path. You can either learn the lessons of independence quickly, through experience, or life will teach you those lessons in its own, often more difficult, way. Life is short, and the quicker we adapt to its harsh realities, the sooner we can move forward with purpose and growth. This can only be achieved when we set out on our own journey, equipped with the guidance and wisdom of our parents. While they will always be there to offer support and advice, the journey itself must be undertaken by you. Ultimately, it is an individual's responsibility to decide what they want from life, chart their own course, and pursue a meaningful existence. Independence is not about abandoning those who care for you; it's about learning, growing, and navigating life's challenges on your own terms while still having the safety net of family support. The pursuit of a meaningful life is a personal expedition, and it's up to each person to steer their own boat toward their destination.

Sara's Journey to Independence

Sara grew up in a close-knit Indian family, where expectations were clear from the start: excel in school, pursue a respectable profession—engineering or medicine—and live at home until she married. Her parents had sacrificed a lot to give her the best opportunities, and Sara loved them deeply. But as she grew older, she started feeling suffocated by the expectations placed upon her.

Her passion had always been for the arts—specifically, painting—but pursuing a career in something creative was unimaginable to her parents, who believed it was impractical. They envisioned her following the traditional route of becoming a doctor, just as her older brother had done. Though she tried to explain her dreams to them, they dismissed her aspirations as a "phase" she would grow out of.

After graduating from high school, Sara was accepted into a prestigious medical program. Her parents were elated, but Sara felt torn. The thought of spending the next several years studying something she had no interest in weighed heavily on her. One day, after a long internal struggle, she made the most difficult decision of her life: she told her parents she was moving to another city to attend art school.

The news was not well-received. Her parents were devastated and could not understand why she would give up a stable, well-paying career for something they considered frivolous. They were disappointed, and their disappointment was palpable in every phone call, and every message. Sara felt an enormous sense of guilt, but she knew in her heart that she needed to live life on her own terms.

She moved out, rented a small apartment near the art school, and began her new life. The transition wasn't easy. Money was tight, and for the first time in her life, Sara had to manage everything on her own—cooking, cleaning, and paying bills. On top of that, she had the pressure of proving to herself and her parents that she could succeed in the world of art. There were moments when she questioned her decision, especially when she compared her life to her friends who had followed more conventional paths.

However, as time passed, Sara began to thrive. Living independently gave her a sense of freedom and autonomy she had never experienced before. She had complete control over her life, her schedule, and her choices. She spent her days immersed in her art and even began to receive recognition for her work at school. Her confidence grew, and with it, her ability to handle life's challenges. She also developed a strong support system of friends and mentors who believed in her, something that helped her through the difficult days.

During this period of self-discovery, Sara also began to understand her parents' perspective better. They were products of their upbringing and culture, and their expectations came from a place of love and protection. But Sara realized that in order to honour their sacrifices, she had to forge her own path—not out of defiance, but out of the desire to live a fulfilled authentic life.

After two years of living on her own and pursuing her passion, Sara returned home for a visit. At first, the tension was palpable, but something had shifted. Her parents saw that she had become more mature, self-reliant, and confident. She wasn't the same girl who had left home, uncertain and torn between her dreams and their expectations. Now, she was a young woman who had found her purpose and direction. Her parents, though still not fully understanding her choice, began to respect her more as an independent adult. They saw that she was capable of standing on her own feet. Over time, their relationship improved. Conversations became less about what she "should" be doing and more about what she was accomplishing on her own. Sara's independence had allowed them to develop a new dynamic—one based on mutual respect rather than obligation.

Sara's journey to break free from her parents' expectations wasn't easy, but it was necessary for her growth. Living independently gave her the opportunity to carve out her own identity, away from the pressures of family tradition. While her relationship with her parents had been strained at first, the time apart allowed for healing and understanding. When Sara returned home, she wasn't seeking their approval, but rather sharing her accomplishments and personal growth with them.

Absence had indeed made the heart grow fonder, and her value in the eyes of her parents had increased. They now saw her as a capable, self-reliant adult who had the courage to pursue her dreams. Sara, in turn, appreciated their love and concern more deeply, understanding that true independence doesn't mean rejecting family, but finding a balance between honoring their values and pursuing your own path.

This story highlights the importance of breaking away from parental expectations when they do not align with personal goals. It shows that while the journey to independence can be challenging, it ultimately leads to growth, mutual respect, and a stronger, more meaningful relationship with family.

Marriage and the Pressure to Conform

Marriage is one of the most significant relationships in most people's lives, and it comes with its own set of challenges, especially in cultures where arranged marriages are still common. In India, for instance, the divorce rate is notably low—around 6%—compared to much higher rates in countries like the United States, where nearly 50% of marriages end in divorce. However, this low divorce rate doesn't necessarily indicate happier marriages; it often reflects societal pressures to conform and the tendency to "adjust" rather than address issues. In an arranged marriage, couples often begin their life together before they fully know each other, leading to a period of "testing" where they try to understand each other's personalities, likes, dislikes, and values. Unlike in love marriages, where this exploration happens before commitment, arranged marriages require couples to work through these issues after the fact. While this can lead to deep bonds of compromise and understanding, it can also result in long-term dissatisfaction if partners aren't compatible.

When adjustment turns into self-sacrifice, resentment can build, and one partner may begin to feel like they are carrying the burden of the relationship. In such cases, it's essential to ask yourself whether the relationship is truly serving your happiness. If the answer is no, it may be time to reassess the situation. Staying in an unhappy relationship due to societal pressure can lead to a lifetime of regret.

Navigating Toxic Marriages

If your marriage is toxic, or if your partner consistently undermines your well-being, the situation can feel hopeless. In some cases, the emotional toll of staying in a toxic marriage can be greater than the fear of leaving it. However, the decision to leave a marriage—especially when children are involved—is never easy. It requires immense courage and careful consideration. any decision that alters your life completely needs to be made with careful consideration.

We often have a tendency to justify our own actions, thoughts, or decisions based on our intentions—essentially, we expect others to understand the reasons behind what we do, even if the outcomes don't always align with our original goals. When we make a choice or take an action, we usually know our intent—what we hoped to achieve, the thought process behind it, and the emotions driving us. In our minds, these intentions provide a justification for our actions, making us feel justified or validated in what we've done. This internal justification stems from the belief that, if others understood our true intentions, they would see the "good" or positive purpose behind our behavior, even if the results are not as intended.

However, we tend to view others' actions or words differently. We often judge others not by their intentions but by the visible outcomes of what they say or do. If someone's words or actions hurt us, we are less likely to empathize with their reasons behind it. Instead, we focus on how their behavior affects us or others in the immediate moment. This creates a kind of double standard where we expect others to give us the benefit of the doubt regarding our good intentions, but we might not extend the same understanding to others, particularly if their actions don't align with our expectations.

This difference in perspective can lead to misunderstandings and conflicts. While we may feel that our intentions should be enough to explain our actions, others might only see the outcome or the way something was said, which might not match the good intentions we had in mind. In relationships, whether personal or professional, this discrepancy can create tension, as each party may feel misunderstood or unfairly judged.

The key to bridging this gap lies in recognizing that intentions are important, but actions and words carry weight as well. While our good intentions should ideally be acknowledged, it's equally important to communicate them effectively and be mindful of the impact our behavior has on others. At the same time, we need to make an effort to consider the intentions behind the actions and words of others, understanding that they, too, may have had positive motives even if the results weren't as intended. By cultivating empathy and practicing open, compassionate communication, we can create a more balanced and understanding environment where both intentions and actions are given fair consideration.

Thinking for yourself involves not only self-reflection and decision-making but also understanding and balancing your emotions and logical reasoning. When you think with your emotions, you are often guided by how you feel in the moment—your desires, fears, and experiences. Emotions can be a powerful force, providing you with passion, motivation, and empathy, but they can also cloud judgment, especially in challenging situations. Emotional thinking is often subjective and can lead to impulsive decisions based on short-term gratification or fear. While emotions can help you understand your needs and connect with others, relying solely on them may result in choices that are not always in your best interest.

On the other hand, thinking through logic involves using reason, facts, and analysis to make decisions. Logic is objective, and it helps you weigh options, predict consequences, and evaluate risks and benefits. It brings clarity and structure to decision-making, particularly in situations where emotions might distort your view. Logical thinking allows you to consider long-term goals and think critically about the consequences of your actions. It helps create a sense of control and confidence, providing you with the ability to navigate complex problems.

However, the most effective thinking involves a combination of both emotional and logical approaches. Emotional awareness can provide insight into your true desires and values, while logic helps you process those feelings and determine the best course of action. Thinking for yourself means acknowledging your emotions and using them as a guide, but also allowing logic to refine those emotions into clear, rational decisions. This approach helps you stay true to your inner self, while also considering the practical realities of the world around you.

Additionally, thinking for others involves stepping beyond your personal feelings and understanding their perspectives, often through logical analysis. It's about considering their emotions, needs, and desires in a rational way that helps them create more harmonious relationships and make decisions that are beneficial for everyone involved. Logical thinking allows you to empathize with others while still maintaining a clear view of the situation, creating balanced decisions that are considerate of both your own emotions and those of others. By learning to navigate the balance between emotional and logical thinking, you can make decisions that are both heartfelt and well-reasoned, ensuring a more thoughtful and effective approach to life's challenges.

Extra-marital affairs, often seen as a step towards finding solace or escape from an unhappy marriage, tend only to intensify the existing issues. Rather than addressing the root causes of dissatisfaction within the marriage, infidelity introduces a new set of complications, such as guilt, betrayal, and emotional turmoil. It creates additional emotional baggage that complicates the relationship further, making it harder to resolve underlying problems. When someone seeks external validation through an affair, they may believe it offers a temporary solution or relief, but in reality, it simply sidesteps the need to confront the true issues at hand.

It is crucial first to face the reality of your current relationship and assess whether it is possible to restore it. This means having open, honest communication with your partner, seeking counseling, or, in some cases, considering separation to allow space for reflection and growth. Only by confronting the situation directly and with sincerity can one determine the next steps. Adding another layer of problems through infidelity before addressing the foundational issues in the relationship will not provide any long-term resolution. Instead, it often leads to more emotional pain, mistrust, and further distance between partners. A thoughtful and proactive approach, rooted in honest communication and mutual effort, is essential before taking any drastic steps that could deepen the divide in your relationship.

Emily's Struggle with a Toxic Relationship

Emily had been in a relationship with her boyfriend, Jake, for five years. What had started as a whirlwind romance, filled with passion and excitement, slowly morphed into something far more draining and unhealthy. Jake was charming at first, but over time, his true nature began to reveal itself. He became increasingly controlling, criticizing Emily's decisions, questioning her every move, and isolating her from her friends and family. Whenever she tried to address her concerns, Jake would manipulate the situation, making Emily feel like she was being overly sensitive or irrational.

Despite the red flags, Emily stayed in the relationship for years. She believed that if she just worked harder or loved him more, things would get better. She also feared what life would be like without Jake—after all, five years is a long time, and she had grown accustomed to having him in her life, even if it wasn't a healthy relationship. She often thought about leaving, but the fear of starting over, coupled with Jake's constant gaslighting, made her doubt her own judgment.

One day, Emily confided in her best friend, Sarah, about the situation. Sarah had been noticing the changes in Emily for a while—she had become quieter, more withdrawn, and had stopped participating in activities she once loved. When Emily finally opened up about the emotional manipulation and control she had been experiencing, Sarah listened without judgment. For the first time, Emily felt seen and heard.

That conversation was a turning point for Emily. Sarah gently reminded her that love shouldn't feel like a burden, and that true love is built on respect, trust, and mutual support. She encouraged Emily to reflect on the relationship and ask herself if it was truly helping her grow or if it was holding her back.

After much contemplation, Emily realized that staying with Jake wasn't love—it was fear. She feared being alone and feared that maybe Jake was right about her being "too difficult" or "too emotional." But deep down, she knew that she deserved better, even if it meant facing the pain of walking away.

One evening, after yet another argument where Jake belittled her for expressing her feelings, Emily made the decision to leave. She packed a bag and walked out, not knowing exactly where she was headed but knowing that staying was no longer an option. It was one of the hardest decisions she had ever made, but in that moment, she felt a sense of liberation she hadn't experienced in years.

The weeks that followed were tough. Emily questioned her decision many times, especially when Jake would send her messages, apologizing and promising to change. But every time she thought about going back, she reminded herself of the years of emotional exhaustion and manipulation she had endured. She knew deep down that while leaving was painful, staying would have been far worse in the long run.

After breaking away from Jake, Emily took time to heal. She reconnected with old friends, started attending therapy, and began focusing on her own needs and desires—things she had neglected for far too long. As time passed, she realized how much of herself she had lost in the relationship. She had sacrificed her happiness and self-worth just to keep the peace.

In therapy, Emily learned that toxic relationships often operate on cycles of control, manipulation, and dependency. She began to understand that Jake's behavior was not her fault and that no amount of love or patience could change someone who was unwilling to change themselves. This realization was key in helping her move forward. The more distance she put between herself and the relationship, the clearer it became how much Jake had stunted her growth. She was no longer weighed down by his constant criticisms or need for control. She started exploring new hobbies, traveling, and setting boundaries in all areas of her life—something she had struggled with for years. Most importantly, Emily rediscovered her own strength. Breaking away from Jake wasn't just about leaving a bad relationship; it was about reclaiming her life and her sense of self-worth. It was about realizing that she didn't need someone else to validate her or make her feel whole. She was enough, just as she was.

As Emily continued to heal, she began to thrive in ways she never thought possible. She returned to her love of painting, a passion Jake had always dismissed as "childish." She took up yoga and meditation to help ground herself and find inner peace. Slowly but surely, she began to rebuild her life on her own terms, free from the emotional chains that had once held her captive.

Her relationship with herself became the most important relationship in her life. She learned how to listen to her own needs, how to set boundaries with others, and how to walk away from situations that didn't serve her. She also learned that it's okay to be alone, and that solitude can be empowering, not something to fear. Breaking away from Jake had been the catalyst for profound personal growth. What had once seemed like an insurmountable obstacle became the doorway to a life of freedom, self-love, and genuine happiness.

Emily's story is a testament to the power of breaking away from toxic relationships. While it's never easy to walk away from someone you love, staying in a toxic environment will only continue to erode your sense of self. True love and healthy relationships are built on mutual respect, kindness, and support. If a relationship diminishes your self-worth, stifles your growth, or makes you feel small, it's a sign that it's time to walk away.

Breaking free from toxic relationships isn't just about escaping negativity—it's about reclaiming your life, your happiness, and your potential. It's about choosing yourself, even when it's hard, and recognizing that you deserve to be treated with love, respect, and care. By walking away, you open the door to healing, growth, and the chance to build a life that reflects your true worth.

The role of children in relationships adds a significant layer of complexity to the dynamics between partners, especially when faced with challenges like separation or divorce. When children are involved, the stakes are inherently higher, as their emotional well-being is deeply intertwined with the stability and health of the relationship between their parents. Children, particularly at younger ages, are highly sensitive to the changes in their environment, and parental separation or conflict can have lasting emotional consequences. They may struggle with feelings of confusion, insecurity, and sadness, which can manifest in behavioral issues, difficulties in school, and strained relationships with both parents. The impact of these emotional shifts can extend well into adulthood, shaping how children form their own relationships and view family dynamics.

The Role of Children in Relationships

Before making any significant decisions regarding the future of a marriage, it is essential to consider not only the current state of the relationship but also the potential consequences for the children involved. This includes taking into account their emotional resilience and capacity to adapt to significant life changes. Ideally, decisions should be made with their best interests in mind, ensuring that their needs for security, stability, and emotional support are prioritized.

One critical factor to consider is the timing of having children. Having children during a period of relationship uncertainty can complicate matters, as it may place additional stress on both partners and the overall family dynamic. Waiting until both partners feel secure in their relationship and are confident in their ability to provide a stable, loving environment can prevent unnecessary complications down the line. Children thrive in environments where they feel safe and loved, and their emotional and psychological development is directly influenced by the quality of the relationships around them. When parents are able to offer a solid foundation of trust, communication, and cooperation, children are more likely to flourish.

The ultimate priority should always be to create a stable, nurturing environment for children, as they are incredibly impressionable and rely heavily on their parents for emotional guidance. Whether parents decide to stay together or separate, it's essential that both parents work collaboratively to ensure the children's needs are met and that they are shielded from any unnecessary distress. The decision-making process should focus on what is best for the family unit as a whole, keeping in mind that children's emotional security must remain at the forefront.

Final say: Eliminate Toxicity, Embrace Growth

The key takeaway from understanding relationships—whether with family, friends, or partners—is that toxicity must be eliminated for true personal growth to occur. Surround yourself with people who uplift you, who share your values, and who contribute positively to your journey. The process of eliminating toxic relationships is never easy, but it is the first and most crucial step toward living a life of peace, joy, and fulfillment.

The courage to break free from toxic relationships is the beginning of a new chapter, one where you can focus on your personal growth, happiness, and well-being. Relationships, when nurtured with care and intention, can be one of life's greatest sources of joy, but only if they are built on mutual respect, love, and shared growth.

In the next chapter, we are going to see how the elimination method can be applied to Money, which will take you to the path of being wealthy.

CHAPTER FOUR

MONEY

Weren't you surprised when we ended the last chapter with the notion that elimination could make you wealthy?

The question arises: how can eliminating money lead to wealth?

The answer lies not in removing money but in understanding its mechanics and eliminating habits, expenses, or investments that keep you perpetually poor. While growing up, many of us noticed our parents being meticulous about their spending, saving diligently for uncertain times through avenues like fixed deposits or gold. Their mindset was shaped by experiences of economic instability during periods of wars and recessions. This survival-oriented approach—saving for an uncertain future—has been ingrained in human behavior for generations. In regions prone to natural disasters, for instance, communities have long stored resources in safer areas to mitigate risks.

Our ancestors developed these practices to navigate uncertain times, but modern generations, such as Millennials and Gen Z, have grown up in relatively stable environments. They haven't witnessed global conflicts like World Wars I and II. Instead, they've embraced the "YOLO" (You Only Live Once) philosophy, prioritizing immediate gratification over long-term security. Today's youth often take on credit card debt or personal loans to finance luxuries like the latest gadgets or high-end bikes. This "spend-before-you-earn" culture has rapidly gained traction over the past few decades, reflecting a stark contrast with older generations who prioritized saving and building wealth during uncertain times.

The absence of large-scale conflicts for several decades led to a perception of continuous economic growth. Many believed their income streams were secure, fueling a mindset of constant consumption. However, the COVID-19 pandemic shattered this illusion. It reminded the world that economies can contract and income streams can dry up, leaving those without savings or emergency funds vulnerable. This realization prompted a global shift towards saving and investing, with many turning to stock markets and mutual funds. The influx of retail investors rejuvenated markets, and rising indices fueled optimism among new investors. However, this optimism often led to over-investment, with people exceeding their risk tolerance in the hope of quick wealth. Stories of young millionaires promoted on social media only deepened this illusion of perpetual growth.

While hope for a better tomorrow is essential, we must recognize that progress often involves temporary instability. Are we prepared for the next **"Black Swan"** event—a rare and unpredictable crisis with severe consequences? Preparation involves building emergency funds, diversifying investments, and understanding financial risks. As author Nassim Nicholas Taleb emphasizes, decentralizing resources can mitigate the impact of such events. While this might seem contradictory to earlier discussions about focus, the key is balancing focused efforts with a diversified approach. For example, Tata Group didn't build its empire overnight but started with Tata Steel and gradually diversified into multiple industries. This strategy created a recession-proof ecosystem where underperforming sectors are offset by thriving ones. Individuals, too, can adopt this approach by gradually adding income streams and investments to their portfolios, ensuring resilience during economic downturns.

For most people, the goal isn't to build an empire like the Tatas or Ambanis but to achieve financial independence—a life where money no longer dictates decisions. Achieving this requires disciplined saving and investing, particularly in the face of rapid inflation and economic uncertainty. Governments offer retirement schemes, but many find these insufficient to sustain a comfortable lifestyle. Additionally, workplace stress has driven some to pursue early retirement, saving aggressively but sometimes overexposing themselves to high-risk assets. With geopolitical tensions escalating—such as the Israel-Iran conflict and the ongoing Russia-Ukraine war—the global economy is under strain. The looming threat of World War

III underscores the need for financial preparedness.

Financial Freedom

Achieving financial independence requires a clear plan and disciplined execution. In the following sections, we will explore the 7 Principles of Financial Freedom, which provide actionable guidance for managing resources effectively, navigating risks, and securing long-term financial well-being. Let's dive in!

1. Spend Less Than You Earn

The foundation of financial freedom is simple: live within your means. If your expenses regularly exceed your income, debt accumulates, and financial stress mounts. Budgeting is crucial here. It allows you to track your spending and ensure you are consistently saving. As your income grows, maintaining this principle ensures that you are putting money aside for future needs rather than succumbing to lifestyle inflation.

2. Create and Stick to a Budget

A budget serves as your financial blueprint. It helps you allocate money towards essential expenses, savings, investments, and discretionary spending. Sticking to a budget helps avoid impulse purchases and ensures you are prioritizing your financial goals. A well-planned budget also gives you a clear picture of where your money is going, empowering you to make adjustments when needed.

3. Build an Emergency Fund

Unexpected expenses are inevitable, whether they come in the form of medical bills, car repairs, or job loss. An emergency fund acts as a safety net to prevent financial setbacks from becoming crises. Financial experts often recommend saving 3 to 6 months' worth of living expenses. This cushion provides peace of mind, ensuring you can navigate life's uncertainties without risking financial hardship or falling into debt.

4. Pay Off Debt

Debt, particularly high-interest debt, can be a major barrier to financial freedom. Paying off debt should be a top priority. Start by tackling high-interest debts, such as credit card balances, before moving on to lower-interest loans like student loans or mortgages. Strategies like the "debt snowball" (paying off small debts first) or "debt avalanche" (paying off high-interest debts first) can help you stay motivated and systematic in eliminating debt.

5. Invest for the Future

Building wealth over time requires more than just saving—it requires investing. Begin by contributing to retirement accounts. If your employer offers a match on retirement contributions, take full advantage of it—it's essentially free money. Beyond retirement, diversify your investments across stocks, bonds, real estate, or other assets based on your risk tolerance and time horizon. The earlier you start investing, the more you can benefit from compound interest.

6. Protect Your Assets

Financial freedom isn't just about accumulating wealth; it's also about protecting it. This includes having the right insurance coverage (health, life, auto, home) and creating an estate plan with wills and trusts. Adequate insurance protects you and your family from financial disaster in the event of unforeseen accidents, illness, or other emergencies.

7. Practice Mindful Spending

Financial freedom doesn't mean denying yourself all pleasures—it means being intentional with your spending. Prioritize spending money on things that align with your values and bring you genuine happiness. Avoid "keeping up with the Joneses" and mindless consumerism, which can erode savings and make financial freedom harder to achieve. Instead, focus on long-term goals and spend on experiences and essentials that contribute to a meaningful life.

These 7 principles form the foundation of financial freedom by emphasizing saving, planning, debt reduction, investment, and mindful decision-making. By following them, individuals can progressively build wealth, eliminate financial stress, and enjoy the flexibility to live life on their own terms.

Since the theme of this book is to Eliminate unnecessarily, I will stress more on the topic of 'Spend Less Than You Earn'. The principle of spending less than you earn is the cornerstone of achieving and maintaining financial freedom. It sounds simple, yet it's one of the most powerful financial habits you can adopt. Here's why it's important, and how to do it effectively:

Living within your means allows you to build savings, avoid debt, and invest in your future. When you consistently spend less than you earn, you create a surplus of income that can be directed toward long-term financial goals, such as saving for retirement, buying a home, or starting a business.

Many people fall into the trap of lifestyle inflation—when income increases, so do expenses. Without discipline, it becomes easy to rationalize higher spending on luxuries or non-essentials as "deserved" rewards. However, this often leaves little room for savings and can lead to financial stress when unexpected expenses arise. By controlling your spending, you free yourself from the paycheck-to-paycheck cycle, allowing for financial flexibility and security. Even modest adjustments in how much you save can have an enormous impact over time, especially when compounded by interest in savings or investment accounts.

How to Spend Less Than You Earn:

Create a Budget: A well-planned budget is essential. Start by tracking your income and expenses. There are many budgeting tools and apps that can help categorize your spending so you can see exactly where your money is going. This gives you a clear view of where to cut back if necessary.

Prioritize Needs Over Wants: Identify essential expenses—such as housing, food, utilities, and healthcare—and make sure these are covered first. Luxuries and discretionary spending (like dining out, entertainment, and vacations) should only be considered once your essentials and savings goals are met.

Avoid Lifestyle Inflation: As your income grows, resist the temptation to upgrade your lifestyle unnecessarily. It's okay to reward yourself but stay mindful of your bigger financial goals. The key is to maintain or slightly adjust your spending habits as your income increases while channeling the extra money into savings and investments.

Automate Savings: One of the best ways to ensure you spend less than you earn is to automate your savings. Set up automatic transfers to your savings or investment accounts each time you get paid. By "paying yourself first," you'll ensure that money is set aside before you're tempted to spend it on non-essentials. Track and Adjust Regularly: Financial situations change over time, so regularly review your budget and spending habits. If you notice an increase in unnecessary spending, take corrective measures. Likewise, if your income increases, consider adjusting your savings targets accordingly.

Eliminating unnecessary expenses is a gradual process, but once it becomes a habit, you'll notice reduced financial stress, increased savings, and the ability to meet your long-term financial goals.

Another important step in financial freedom is 'Pay Off Debt': Freeing Yourself from Financial Burdens Debt is one of the biggest obstacles to achieving financial freedom. High-interest debt, especially from credit cards, can drain your finances and limit your ability to save or invest. This principle emphasizes the importance of making debt repayment a priority, as eliminating debt provides you with more control over your finances and reduces stress.

Why It's Important:

Debt is not just a financial burden—it's a psychological one too. Carrying debt often leads to anxiety, limits your financial flexibility, and can keep you trapped in a cycle of paying interest without making much progress on the principal balance. The longer you carry debt, especially high-interest debt, the more you pay in interest, often making it harder to achieve your financial goals.

By paying off your debts, you're effectively giving yourself a pay raise because more of your money stays with you instead of going toward interest payments. Once you're debt-free, you can redirect the money that was once used for debt repayment into savings, investments, or other wealth-building activities.

How to Pay Off Debt:

List All Debts: The first step to tackling debt is knowing exactly what you owe. List all your debts, including credit cards, student loans, car loans, personal loans, and mortgages. Note the balances, interest rates, and minimum payments for each debt.

Choose a Repayment Strategy: There are two popular strategies for paying off debt:

The Debt Snowball Method: Focus on paying off the smallest debt first, regardless of the interest rate, while making minimum payments on the others. Once the smallest debt is paid off, move on to the next smallest. This method provides quick wins that can build motivation.

The Debt Avalanche Method: Focus on paying off the debt with the highest interest rate first, while making minimum payments on the others. Once the highest-interest debt is eliminated, move on to the next highest. This method saves you the most money in interest over time.

Make Extra Payments When Possible: Any extra income—bonuses, tax refunds, side gigs—should be funneled into debt repayment. Paying more than the minimum reduces the principal faster, saving you money on interest and shortening the life of the loan.

Consolidate or Refinance Debt: If you have multiple high-interest debts, you might consider consolidating them into a single loan with a lower interest rate. Balance transfer credit cards, personal loans, or refinancing options can simplify payments and reduce the total interest paid.

Avoid Taking on New Debt: It's important to stop adding to your debt while you're in the process of paying it off. Avoid credit card use, and resist financing large purchases like cars or vacations until your existing debt is under control.

Celebrate Milestones: Paying off debt is a significant achievement. Celebrate small wins along the way, whether it's paying off a credit card balance or eliminating a student loan. These moments will keep you motivated and committed to your overall financial goals.

The Psychological Benefit of Debt Freedom

Becoming debt-free is not only a financial relief, but it also has a tremendous psychological benefit. It reduces stress, improves your mental well-being, and allows you to focus on future financial goals, such as saving for retirement, investing, or simply enjoying the fruits of your labor.

By freeing yourself from debt, you're no longer working just to pay bills—you're working toward building wealth and achieving true financial freedom.

In summary, the first principle of spending less than you earn establishes the foundation for building savings and wealth, while the fourth principle of paying off debt is crucial for eliminating financial burdens that impede progress. Together, these principles create a powerful pathway toward financial security and independence.

Let's go through the story of Carlos who is representative of the modern generation facing the same kind of problems and understand how he tackled it to have control over his financial situation.

The Wake-Up Call

Meet Carlos, a 35-year-old software engineer who had been earning a good salary for several years but found himself buried in debt. He had a mortgage, credit card debt, and a car loan. Despite his well-paying job, Carlos was constantly stressed about his finances. He lived in a cycle of spending more than he earned, making only the minimum payments on his debt, and relying on his credit cards for everyday expenses. Every month, his balance grew, and the dream of financial freedom seemed farther and farther away.

One day, Carlos received a notification that his credit card had reached its limit. Embarrassed and anxious, he realized he had no room left for emergency expenses and was close to defaulting on his payments. This was his wake-up call. He needed to make a change, and fast. After some research, Carlos learned about two key principles that could be his way out: Spend Less Than You Earn and Pay Off Debt.

Carlos sat down with his bank statements and credit card bills to figure out where his money was going. He was shocked to see how much he was spending on non-essential items—dining out, subscription services, and impulse purchases. His first step was to create a strict budget.

He started by cutting unnecessary expenses. Carlos canceled streaming services, and gym memberships he rarely used, and limited his eating out to once a month. He also made an effort to cook at home, take public transportation instead of driving, and avoid buying things on impulse. This change wasn't easy at first, but Carlos quickly saw the benefits. Within a couple of months, he noticed that he had more money left over at the end of each pay period.

Carlos also took on freelance projects to increase his income. By adding a bit of extra work on weekends, he was able to boost his earnings without drastically changing his daily routine.

With a little extra cash each month, Carlos turned his attention to his debt. He decided to tackle his credit card debt first, as it had the highest interest rate. Using the snowball method, he listed all his debts from smallest to largest, making minimum payments on the larger debts while aggressively paying down the smallest one. Each time he cleared a balance, Carlos felt a small victory. After a few months, he paid off his first credit card. Motivated by the progress, he shifted focus to the next debt on the list—his car loan. By sticking to his budget and resisting the urge to overspend, Carlos continued making extra payments on his debts, one by one.

Carlos also called his credit card company to negotiate a lower interest rate, which helped him reduce the amount of interest he was paying each month. The combination of living below his means, budgeting, and paying off debt systematically allowed him to make consistent progress.

As the months went by, Carlos noticed a significant shift in his financial situation. His debts were shrinking, and his stress levels were decreasing. He had more control over his finances, and the idea of financial freedom didn't seem impossible anymore.

In two years, Carlos had paid off his credit card debt entirely and significantly reduced his car loan. He even managed to put aside some savings for emergencies. As his debts decreased, he also started contributing more to his retirement fund, setting himself up for long-term financial security.

Carlos's journey taught him the value of spending less than you earn and the importance of paying off debt. Once trapped in a cycle of overspending, he realized that small lifestyle adjustments and disciplined debt repayment could drastically improve his financial health.

Today, Carlos is on the path to financial freedom. His new goal is to pay off his mortgage within the next 10 years and build up his investments. By focusing on these two fundamental principles early on, Carlos was able to regain control of his finances and is now confidently planning for a debt-free future.

He often reflects on how different his life is now compared to when he lived paycheck to paycheck. The stress and anxiety over money are gone, replaced by a sense of empowerment and peace. Carlos's story is a testament to how spending less than you earn and paying off debt can be the first, crucial steps to financial freedom.

The Power of Delayed Gratification

In the realm of financial management, delayed gratification is not just a smart strategy—it is the cornerstone of long-term financial success. The ability to resist the urge to spend impulsively in favor of saving or investing leads to financial security, independence, and ultimately, freedom. Here's how delayed gratification plays a pivotal role in everyday financial decisions:

Avoiding Impulse Purchases

Every day, we're bombarded with advertisements and opportunities to spend money—whether it's the latest smartphone, a sale on designer clothes, or a tempting vacation package. These purchases offer instant gratification, giving us a brief thrill or momentary pleasure. However, constantly giving in to these impulses can derail your long-term financial goals.

When you practice delayed gratification, you consciously resist these temptations in favor of something more meaningful. Instead of splurging on a new gadget that you don't need, you might save that money for an emergency fund, a down payment on a house, or retirement. By waiting and weighing the long-term value of a purchase, you prevent yourself from accumulating unnecessary debt and ensure that your money is spent wisely.

Example: Imagine someone who wants the latest iPhone but already has a perfectly functioning phone. Instead of giving in to the excitement of owning the newest model, they wait and allocate that money toward their retirement savings or paying off debt. In the short term, they miss out on the novelty of a new device, but in the long term, they build greater financial security.

The book Psychology of Money is one of my favorite reads, second only to Poor Economics by Nobel Prize winner Amartya Sen. Both books delve into the contrasting ways wealthy and poor people perceive and manage money. For the wealthy, money serves as a tool to buy time, enabling them to focus on activities that generate further wealth and provide freedom. In contrast, the poor often use money to purchase liabilities—things that not only fail to generate income but also demand more of their time and energy. This often traps them in what can be termed modern-day slavery: the relentless cycle of working in a job they may not enjoy, just to pay off debts.

The wealthy invest in assets and create income streams that allow them to think strategically, explore opportunities, and build more resources. On the other hand, the poor, driven by immediate desires, frequently incur new debts to fulfill temporary wants, further entrenching themselves in a cycle of financial instability. This mindset perpetuates a debt trap, making it exceedingly difficult for individuals with a poor financial mentality to break free and achieve lasting prosperity.

The Power of Compounding: A Financial Superpower

Compounding is often described as the most powerful force in finance and one of the most effective wealth-building tools available. Albert Einstein is famously (and perhaps apocryphally) credited with calling compound interest the "eighth wonder of the world." He allegedly said, "He who understands it, earns it; he who doesn't, pays it." This quote highlights the transformative potential of compounding when harnessed wisely, as well as its consequences when ignored.

At its core, compounding occurs when the returns on an initial investment are reinvested, allowing subsequent returns to grow not only on the original principal but also on the accumulated gains. Over time, this creates a snowball effect where the growth accelerates exponentially. The longer the time horizon, the more pronounced the impact of compounding. This is why starting early, even with modest amounts, can lead to extraordinary outcomes.

For example, consider an investment of $1,000 earning an annual return of 10%. After one year, it grows to $1,100. If the $100 in gains is reinvested, the investment grows to $1,210 in the second year, $1,331 in the third year, and so on. By the 20th year, the initial $1,000 becomes over $6,700—not because more money was added, but because the gains were reinvested and allowed to grow on themselves.

The key ingredient in compounding is time. The earlier you start and the longer you let your investments grow, the greater the potential benefits. This is why compounding is often referred to as "earning money while you sleep." Warren Buffett, one of the world's most successful investors, credits much of his wealth to the power of compounding over decades of disciplined investing.

However, compounding isn't limited to finances. Its principles apply to knowledge, relationships, and habits. Small, consistent efforts in any area of life accumulate and can lead to massive results over time.

Conversely, compounding can work against you if you're not mindful. High-interest debt, such as credit card balances, can create a compounding effect in the opposite direction, trapping individuals in a cycle of ever-growing liabilities.

In summary, compounding is a remarkable phenomenon that rewards patience and consistency. It underscores the value of starting early, staying disciplined, and giving your investments—and your efforts—the time they need to grow exponentially. Einstein's observation about compound interest reminds us to respect its power, whether earning or paying it.

The elimination method can be a transformative approach for helping individuals break free from the poverty trap. At its core, this method involves identifying and removing the habits, behaviors, and financial practices that perpetuate poverty, enabling individuals to redirect their limited resources toward creating long-term stability and growth.

One of the primary reasons many people remain stuck in poverty is the misallocation of resources. For example, spending on non-essential items, high-interest loans, or short-term gratifications drains their limited income, leaving little room for savings or investments. By eliminating unnecessary expenses—such as impulsive purchases or reliance on high-cost borrowing—individuals can start to free up funds to meet essential needs and build a financial cushion.

Elimination also applies to time and energy. People in poverty often spend significant time on activities that yield low or no returns, such as excessive entertainment or unproductive habits. By cutting out these distractions and focusing on skill development, networking, or side hustles, they can begin to increase their income potential and open doors to better opportunities.

Furthermore, eliminating a mindset of helplessness or entitlement is crucial. A scarcity mindset often traps individuals in a cycle of despair, where they believe their circumstances cannot change. Shifting to a growth-oriented mindset—focused on building skills, improving financial literacy, and taking ownership of their future—can unlock the motivation needed to break free from the poverty cycle.

Ultimately, the elimination method is not about deprivation but about making conscious choices to remove what does not serve a person's long-term goals. This creates room for saving, investing, and building a foundation for financial independence. By consistently eliminating what holds them back, individuals can gradually climb out of poverty and work toward a stable and prosperous future.

In the next chapter, we will learn how to apply the elimination method to make work meaningful.

CHAPTER FIVE

WORK

Work is an essential part of our lives, shaping not only our daily routines but also our sense of purpose and personal fulfillment. For many, it consumes the majority of our time, with an average workday now stretching from 9 to 10 hours, and in some industries, even more. It's a reality that has evolved significantly over the years, from physically demanding labor in the early industrial age to today's largely mental and technological work.

Before the rise of information technology, much of the workforce was engaged in manual labor, repetitive and physically taxing jobs, often in factories or farms. People worked long hours, but their work was more physical and direct, with clear outputs of their effort, such as a finished product or a harvested crop. The focus was on mechanical efficiency, not intellectual engagement. Workers were performing the same tasks daily with minimal variation, requiring minimal mental energy.

Shift to Knowledge-Based Work

In the modern era, the landscape of work has changed dramatically. We have moved from industrial labor to knowledge-based work, where mental effort is the key currency. The advent of computers, the internet, and technological advancements like artificial intelligence (AI) and machine learning (ML) have transformed the workplace into a more intellectually demanding space. People are no longer just performing repetitive physical tasks but are solving complex problems, innovating, and contributing creative solutions.

However, this shift has also created new challenges. The boundary between work and personal life has become increasingly blurred, especially with the widespread adoption of remote work following the COVID-19 pandemic. Work-from-home (WFH) has become the norm for millions, and while it offers flexibility and eliminates commutes, it also invades the sanctity of our personal spaces. Bedrooms, kitchens, and living rooms have been repurposed as workspaces, diluting the mental separation between home life and professional responsibilities.

The Blurring of Work and Personal Space

In recent years, the lines between professional and personal life have increasingly blurred, leading to profound psychological effects and challenges for individuals working from home. This overlap transforms our homes from sanctuaries of relaxation into extensions of the workplace, with significant impacts on mental well-being and job satisfaction.

The Transformation of Home Spaces

Traditionally, our homes served as places of comfort, relaxation, and retreat from the demands of work. The living room was a space to unwind with family or enjoy leisure activities, the kitchen was a hub for shared meals and conversations, and the bedrooms were solely dedicated to rest and relaxation. However, the rise of remote work has altered these roles dramatically:

Living Room as a Workspace: What was once a cozy area for relaxation has now become a backdrop for virtual meetings and Zoom calls. The casual atmosphere of the living room, which provided a mental escape from work, is now intertwined with professional duties, making it challenging to separate work from leisure.

Kitchen as an Office: The kitchen, traditionally a space for cooking and family meals, has morphed into a makeshift office. The kitchen table, once a site for shared meals and conversations, is now cluttered with work materials, laptops, and documents. This shift creates an environment where the boundary between work and home life becomes increasingly blurred.

Bedrooms as Dual-purpose Spaces: Bedrooms, once exclusively for rest, now serve dual functions as both sleeping quarters and workspaces. The presence of a home office setup in the bedroom disrupts the natural association between the space and relaxation, making it harder to "switch off" from work mode.

Psychological Effects of the Overlap

The blending of work and personal spaces can take a heavy toll on mental well-being:

Difficulty in Switching Off: The physical overlap between work and home can make it challenging to mentally disengage from work. The constant presence of work materials and the expectation to be perpetually available erode the ability to fully relax and recharge. The home, once a haven of peace, begins to feel like a battleground where work-related stress intrudes into personal time.

Increased Stress and Burnout: The inability to separate work from personal life contributes to heightened stress and burnout. The constant connectivity to work emails, chats, and tasks

creates an environment where mental rest becomes scarce. The blurring of roles leads to a sense of being perpetually "on duty," which can result in exhaustion and dissatisfaction.

Dissatisfaction with Job and Work Environment: Surveys reveal that over 90% of individuals who work from home report feeling disconnected from their jobs and dissatisfied with the blending of work and life. This dissatisfaction often leads individuals to seek alternative income streams or contemplate career changes. However, the prospect of returning to a traditional office setting is equally daunting for many, given the associated stressors such as commuting, workplace politics, and rigid structures.

Navigating the New Paradigm

To address the challenges posed by the blurring of work and personal spaces, individuals and organizations need to adopt strategies that promote balance and well-being:

Establish Clear Boundaries: Create distinct physical and mental boundaries between work and personal life. Designate specific areas of the home for work and others for relaxation. Establish regular work hours and adhere to them, ensuring that work tasks do not encroach upon personal time.

Create a Dedicated Workspace: Set up a dedicated workspace that is separate from areas associated with leisure and relaxation. This helps in maintaining a clear distinction between work and home life and facilitates a better work-life balance.

Prioritize Mental Health: Engage in activities that promote mental well-being and relaxation. Incorporate breaks, exercise, and mindfulness practices into the daily routine to counteract the stress associated with the overlap of work and personal spaces.

Communicate Expectations: Clearly communicate expectations with employers and family members regarding availability and work boundaries. Set realistic expectations about response times and availability to reduce the pressure of constant connectivity.

Seek Support: Utilize available resources and support systems, such as counseling services or employee assistance programs, to address feelings of burnout and dissatisfaction.

Jennifer's Remote Work Success Story

Jennifer, a project manager, faced a different challenge while working remotely—keeping herself motivated and engaged without the structure of an office. She often felt the urge to work beyond normal hours or check her email during family time. This created friction with her work-life balance, and she started to feel burned out.

Jennifer decided to implement strict boundaries. She set up a small desk in a separate room as her workspace and made it a point to only do work there. She also created an end-of-day ritual, where she would clear her desk, close the door, and spend 30 minutes doing yoga to unwind. On weekends, she completely disconnected from work by turning off her work phone and laptop.

This change allowed Jennifer to separate her work and personal life, giving her time to recharge while maintaining her productivity. Over time, she found that she enjoyed remote work more and was able to fully engage in her family life without feeling tethered to her job.

The Collision of Market and Social Norms

In his book "Predictably Irrational," Dan Ariely delves into the fascinating interplay between market norms and social norms, illustrating how these two frameworks can sometimes clash and create complex challenges in our daily lives. Understanding this collision is crucial, especially in modern work environments where the boundaries between professional and personal life are increasingly blurred.

Market Norms vs. Social Norms

To grasp the collision between market and social norms, it helps to first understand what each term represents:

Market Norms: These norms are transactional and are driven by economic incentives. They involve an exchange of goods or services for money or other tangible rewards. In a market norm, actions are performed with the expectation of a clear, often monetary, return. For example, when you work a 40-hour week, you expect a paycheck in return. The relationship is straightforward: work in exchange for compensation.

Social Norms: In contrast, social norms are based on relationships and emotional satisfaction. They involve actions motivated by goodwill, mutual respect, or emotional connections, without the expectation of immediate returns. For instance, you might help a friend move or lend a hand in a community event simply because you care about them or believe in the cause, not because you expect a fiinancial reward.

In social norms, people are motivated by relationships, goodwill, and emotional satisfaction, rather than financial gain. These norms emphasize the value of contributing to a community, helping others, and fostering a sense of belonging. For example, someone may gladly volunteer their time and expertise for a charity without expecting any compensation. The motivation here is purely altruistic—the person feels good knowing they are helping others and making a positive impact.

Let's consider David, a graphic designer. On weekends, David volunteers his time to create flyers and promotional materials for a local charity that supports homeless shelters. He works tirelessly on these projects, spending hours on designs, and is happy to do so because he believes in the cause and feels a sense of personal fulfillment. For David, working for the charity aligns with social norms—he's contributing to something he cares about, and the emotional reward of helping the community is enough.

However, when David performs the same work in his professional life as a graphic designer for clients, the dynamic changes entirely. Here, market norms come into play. David is no longer working out of goodwill or personal satisfaction—he's providing a service that has monetary value. In this setting, David demands compensation because his time and expertise are tied to financial worth. When working for paying clients, David negotiates contracts, sets clear deadlines, and expects to be compensated fairly for his skills. His work under market norms is governed by transactions, where each party expects something tangible in return—money for services rendered.

This illustrates how the same person can approach the same task—creating graphic designs—with different expectations based on whether they are operating under social norms or market norms. In social norms, David works for free because the motivation is emotional and based on relationships and community. In market norms, however, he expects payment because the context shifts to a transactional relationship where his time and skill are commodities with financial value.

This difference in expectations highlights how the same work can be valued differently depending on whether it falls within a social or market framework. It also explains why blending these two norms—like asking someone to volunteer for charity work and then expecting them to apply the same effort to a paying client without compensation—can create confusion and conflict.

When managers at work blur the lines between social norms and market norms, it often creates confusion and tension in the workplace. This happens when a manager taps into the emotional and relational aspects of social norms—like teamwork, loyalty, and goodwill—to get extra work done without offering any tangible compensation, while employees expect the relationship to be governed by market norms, where effort is rewarded with pay, bonuses, or other benefits.

Let's consider an example to illustrate this confusion

Emma works as a project manager at a tech firm. Her job is demanding, and like many professionals, she sees her work primarily through the lens of market norms—she gets paid for the hours she works, and her salary compensates her for her skills and expertise. This relationship is transactional: Emma offers her time, knowledge, and effort, and in return, she receives a paycheck.

One Friday afternoon, Emma's manager, Mike, asks her to stay late and help with an urgent project. But instead of offering overtime pay, comp time, or even a financial bonus, Mike appeals to Emma's sense of social norms. He says things like, "We're all in this together," and "The team really needs you right now." Mike implies that Emma should go the extra mile because of her loyalty to the team and her personal investment in the company's success. However, Emma feels that she's already fulfilled her responsibilities for the week and expects her extra efforts to be compensated.

The Confusion

Here's where the confusion lies. Emma is operating under market norms—she views her work in terms of hours worked for money earned. She expects that if she is asked to put in extra effort, there will be a market-based reward, such as overtime pay, a bonus, or a promotion.

On the other hand, Mike is trying to tap into social norms—he's asking Emma to stay late out of a sense of commitment to the team, the company, and her colleagues. He's asking her to give her time and effort for free, driven by emotional and relational factors like loyalty, camaraderie, and shared responsibility.

The result? Confusion and frustration. Emma is conflicted. On the one hand, she values her job and wants to be a good team player. On the other hand, she feels taken advantage of because she expects her time to be compensated in accordance with market norms. She ends up feeling that the company is benefiting from her generosity without giving anything in return.

The Emotional Fallout

When managers mix social norms and market norms, employees can feel manipulated. By appealing to emotions like loyalty and team spirit, managers may get extra work out of employees in the short term, but over time, this tactic can lead to resentment. Employees may feel that their goodwill is being exploited, especially if there is no formal recognition or reward for their extra efforts. Over time, this can lead to burnout, decreased job satisfaction, and ultimately, higher turnover rates as employees feel undervalued.

The Long-Term Impact

This confusion can have a negative impact on workplace culture. When employees consistently feel that their time and effort are not being properly compensated, they may become less willing to give that extra effort in the future. They might start to disengage, only doing the bare minimum required by their job descriptions. The disconnect between the emotional appeal of social norms and the transactional expectations of market norms leads to a breakdown in trust between employees and management.

In market norms, workers expect to be paid fairly for the value they bring to the company. They understand the exchange: effort for compensation. However, when managers blur the line by using social norms—such as asking for personal favors or extra work based on team loyalty—without providing compensation or acknowledgment, it creates confusion and dissatisfaction.

The confusion between social norms and market norms in the workplace often leads to mixed signals and frustration for employees. While social norms—like teamwork, loyalty, and camaraderie—can foster a positive work environment, they should not be used to replace fair compensation and clear expectations set by market norms. Employees deserve clarity on when their contributions are governed by emotional investments and when they are based on transactional, market-based exchanges. Blending the two can lead to burnout, disengagement, and mistrust in the long run. Clear communication and a proper balance between both norms are essential to maintaining a healthy, productive workplace

The Power of Elimination

One of the most effective strategies to handle work pressure is elimination, not in the sense of avoiding responsibilities but focusing on removing unnecessary or unproductive tasks. Often, people respond to overwhelming work pressure by taking time off or "escaping" the situation. While this may provide temporary relief, it doesn't solve the underlying issue. The real solution lies in identifying what's truly important and eliminating the rest.

This method encourages individuals to streamline their tasks and focus on what adds the most value. Instead of falling into the trap of escapism, where problems are avoided, embracing the elimination approach means confronting challenges head-on. By eliminating redundant or unnecessary tasks, we free up mental space for more creative, fulfilling work.

Taking regular breaks is also crucial, not to avoid work, but to recharge. Planned vacations or time off to rejuvenate are necessary for maintaining productivity and creativity in the long run. However, it's important to delegate tasks or set up systems to ensure that the workflow doesn't come to a standstill in your absence. That way, you can return to work without facing an overwhelming backlog.

Dependency and Loss Aversion

In the workplace, many people create dependencies as a form of job security. They withhold knowledge or keep tasks to themselves, ensuring that they remain indispensable. This behavior is driven by a psychological phenomenon called loss aversion — the tendency to prefer avoiding losses over acquiring gains. Workers fear that if they delegate too much, they will be seen as replaceable.

However, this mentality can backfire. By holding on to repetitive, mundane tasks, workers limit their growth and creativity. In the long run, jobs that involve repetitive work are at risk of being automated by AI and ML technologies. To thrive in the modern workplace, it's important to focus on creative, high-value tasks that showcase your unique skills and abilities. Sharing knowledge and delegating tasks not only frees you up for more important work but also enhances team productivity and collaboration.

A scarcity mindset

Rooted in the belief that resources like money, opportunities, or success are limited, can profoundly affect career decisions and mental well-being. People operating under this mindset often feel trapped in their current jobs, fearing that leaving or exploring new opportunities might result in financial insecurity or professional failure. This fear leads to a cycle of stress and stagnation, perpetuating a sense of helplessness.

When someone believes there are few viable alternatives to their current job, they may avoid taking risks, such as seeking new roles, negotiating better terms, or pursuing additional skills that could open new doors. Instead, they cling tightly to what they have, prioritizing job security over personal growth or fulfillment. This behavior is often fueled by past experiences of instability or uncertainty, such as growing up in a financially strained household or witnessing layoffs in their industry. The fear of losing their livelihood becomes overwhelming, narrowing their perspective on what is possible.

In the workplace, this mindset can lead to overwork, burnout, and an inability to establish healthy boundaries. Employees with a scarcity mindset may feel they must say yes to every task, work excessive hours, or constantly prove their worth to avoid being deemed replaceable. Paradoxically, this overexertion can diminish performance over time, increasing the risk of mistakes, fatigue, and strained relationships with colleagues or managers. The resulting stress reinforces their fear, creating a vicious cycle that can be difficult to break.

Scarcity thinking also dampens creativity and problem-solving abilities. When individuals are consumed by thoughts of survival, their focus shifts to short-term gains rather than long-term strategies. They may struggle to envision alternative career paths, innovative ideas, or entrepreneurial ventures because the fear of losing what they already have overshadows their ability to explore the unknown.

Breaking free from a scarcity mindset requires a shift toward an abundance mentality—believing that opportunities are plentiful and within reach with effort and adaptability. This involves investing in personal development, such as acquiring new skills, networking, and seeking mentors. Building an emergency fund can also provide a financial cushion, reducing immediate fears of job loss. Over time, adopting this perspective allows individuals to approach their work with confidence, set boundaries, and make choices aligned with their values and aspirations rather than fear. By transitioning from scarcity to abundance, people can unlock greater career potential and a sense of freedom in their professional lives.

Embracing Creativity and Innovation

One of the best ways to stay relevant in the evolving job market is to focus on creativity and innovation. In the famous quote attributed to Abraham Lincoln, "If I had eight hours to chop down a tree, I'd spend six hours sharpening my axe," we see the value of preparation and strategic thinking. Instead of grinding away at repetitive tasks, it's far more efficient to invest time in creating systems that streamline work.

For instance, if you're repeatedly performing the same task, why not create a template or automate the process? This upfront effort may take extra time initially, but it will save countless hours in the future. Asking yourself, "How can I eliminate this repetitive task?" encourages innovation and efficiency.

Focus on skill-building

Taking time out from daily work to focus on skill-building is essential for long-term career success, personal growth, and adaptability in an ever-changing world. While routine work fulfills immediate responsibilities, investing time in developing new skills or enhancing existing ones ensures that you remain relevant, innovative, and prepared for future challenges.

1. Staying Relevant in a Dynamic Environment

Industries evolve rapidly, driven by advancements in technology, market demands, and global trends. If you don't keep up with these changes, you risk falling behind. Skill-building enables you to stay ahead, ensuring you remain valuable to your organization or better positioned to pursue new opportunities.

2. Enhancing Career Progression

Acquiring new skills often opens doors to promotions, leadership roles, or entirely new career paths. Whether it's mastering data analytics, public speaking, or technical expertise, skill-building equips you with tools that employers value, making you a more competitive candidate for high-growth roles.

3. Boosting Creativity and Problem-Solving

Breaking away from your daily routine allows you to engage in learning that stimulates creativity and enhances problem-solving abilities. Learning a new skill—such as coding, graphic design, or even a second language—provides fresh perspectives that can be applied to existing challenges at work, fostering innovation.

4. Building Confidence

Expanding your skill set increases your self-confidence. As you master new abilities, you become more self-assured in your capabilities, which can lead to improved decision-making and greater willingness to take calculated risks in your career.

5. Reducing Burnout and Enhancing Work-Life Balance

Focusing solely on work without investing in personal growth can lead to burnout. Taking time for skill-building serves as a mental reset, providing a sense of accomplishment and fulfillment beyond your regular job. This renewed energy and perspective can make your work-life balance healthier.

6. Preparing for Uncertainty

The job market is unpredictable, and relying solely on existing skills can be risky. By taking time to upskill, you future-proof your career, preparing yourself for shifts in industry demands or unforeseen challenges like layoffs or economic downturns.

7. Exploring New Passions

Skill-building can also be a way to explore new interests that might develop into hobbies, side hustles, or even a career change. This exploration not only enriches your life but also broadens your options for professional and personal fulfillment.

8. Creating Long-Term Value

Skills are investments that yield lifelong returns. Unlike material possessions that depreciate over time, knowledge and expertise often grow in value, enabling you to navigate challenges, seize opportunities, and make impactful contributions throughout your career.

Staying relevant by continuously updating your skill set is crucial in today's fast-paced and competitive job market. Organizations operate in a business-first environment, where decisions are driven by profitability and not loyalty. No matter how many years you've dedicated to your company, your hard work and loyalty can become irrelevant if you're no longer adding value or generating revenue for the business. Companies won't hesitate to lay you off if you're no longer deemed essential. Conversely, during economic downturns or recessions, the same companies often expect employees to show loyalty by working extra hours and making sacrifices to help weather tough times.

Once the financial storm passes, however, some organizations will still cut ties with employees under the guise of expansion or restructuring, often citing a lack of leadership qualities or alignment with their growth vision. This stark reality reflects the modern work culture, where very few people retire from the same organization where they started their careers.

The Challenge of Staying Relevant

As industries evolve, many employees feel the mounting pressure to learn new skills and stay competitive. For those who struggle to keep up, the resulting stress can lead to burnout, forcing them to leave their roles prematurely. This highlights the need for every professional to create a safety net. Such a safety net could involve learning new skills, building alternate income streams, or planning for a potential career pivot.

Unfortunately, most organizations discourage employees from engaging in pursuits outside their primary job. Terms like "moonlighting" are often used to criticize efforts to create additional income streams. This can be seen as a form of modern-day corporate control, where businesses and governments rely on the middle class to work tirelessly in 9-to-5 jobs, ensuring the continued growth of industries while keeping employees tethered to their roles.

Reflecting on Organizational Growth vs. Personal Growth

It's important to question whether your professional growth is aligned with your organization's growth. For example, companies often report annual growth in stock market valuations of 15-20%, while employees typically see salary increments capped at 10%. Have you ever analyzed your organization's public financial statements? If you compare your financial growth since joining the company to its overall market growth, you might find discrepancies. If your personal financial growth lags far behind, it's time to reconsider your career priorities.

Similarly, consider the amount of time you dedicate to your job. Is your work-life balance acceptable? Are you sacrificing personal time for office work without adequate compensation? Time is an irreplaceable resource, and its value often outweighs money because it is directly tied to your happiness. If your current role doesn't allow you the personal time you need, it might be time to rethink your career path.

Should You Quit Your Job Immediately?

The answer is no. Knee-jerk reactions can lead to adverse consequences, leaving you stranded without a clear path forward. Instead, it's crucial to take a methodical approach to break free from the so-called 9-to-5 slavery. The first step is not to quit your job but to deeply understand the challenges you face and devise a strategic plan to address them.

Begin by focusing on creating parallel sources of income. This provides a safety net, reducing your dependency on a single paycheck. Such planning requires effort, patience, and careful execution to ensure a smooth transition from financial dependency to independence.

Let's now dive deeper into the importance of generating alternate income streams and explore step-by-step strategies to achieve financial freedom while maintaining stability during the transition. The goal is not just to escape the grind but to build a life that offers both security and satisfaction.

Importance of having a parallel source of income

1. Financial Security and Risk Management
Relying solely on a primary job can be risky, especially in volatile economic climates. Creating alternate income streams acts as a safety net, ensuring you can maintain your financial commitments even if your primary income is disrupted. It reduces dependency and provides a buffer during challenging times.

2. Wealth Creation
Alternate income streams can help accelerate wealth creation by increasing your overall earnings. Whether it's investing in stocks, renting out property, freelancing, or starting a small business, the additional income can be channeled into savings, investments, or debt repayment, compounding your financial growth over time.

3. Pursuing Passions and Interests

Taking time out to explore alternate income opportunities often allows you to monetize hobbies or interests. This not only diversifies your earnings but also brings a sense of fulfillment and joy, turning your passions into productive endeavors that complement your primary job.

4. Achieving Financial Independence

Alternate income sources bring you closer to financial independence, where you no longer rely solely on active work to sustain your lifestyle. Passive income streams, like rental income, dividends, or royalties, provide the freedom to choose how you spend your time and energy.

5. Reducing Stress and Building Confidence

The fear of job loss or economic instability can be a significant source of stress. Having alternate income streams reduces this anxiety, giving you greater peace of mind. It also boosts your confidence in your ability to manage finances and take control of your future.

6. Enhancing Skill Sets and Knowledge

Engaging in side projects or entrepreneurial ventures to generate income enhances your skills and broadens your expertise. For example, learning digital marketing for an online business or acquiring financial literacy for investing sharpens your professional and personal capabilities.

7. Building Resilience Against Inflation

As the cost of living rises, a single paycheck may not keep pace with inflation. Alternate sources of income can offset these increases, ensuring you can maintain or even improve your standard of living without overburdening your primary earnings.

8. Flexibility for Life Goals

Additional income can fund significant life goals, like traveling, buying a house, or supporting family needs. It gives you the financial flexibility to pursue dreams without derailing your financial stability or long-term plans.

Knowing Why Before You Start Working

I credit the book 'Start with Why' by 'Simon Sinek' for changing my perspective towards the work. Work politics started to look trivial after

I found the purpose in my work. Knowing the "why" behind any task is fundamental to achieving meaningful and effective results. Understanding the purpose provides clarity and direction, ensuring that your efforts align with a larger goal rather than being arbitrary or misdirected. When you know the "why," you are more likely to stay motivated, as your work becomes connected to a greater sense of purpose, whether personal, organizational, or societal. It allows you to prioritize tasks effectively, filter out distractions, and allocate resources wisely. Moreover, having a clear "why" fosters creativity and problem-solving, as you understand the outcomes you're striving for and can adapt your approach as needed. Without this foundational understanding, even the most diligent efforts can feel aimless, leading to frustration, wasted time, or subpar results. In short, the "why" serves as a compass, guiding your actions toward meaningful and impactful contributions.

The story of the two bricklayers is often attributed to a real-life event that took place in Europe during the construction of one of the grand medieval cathedrals, though its exact origins remain unclear. It has since been widely used as a parable to illustrate the power of purpose in work.

During the construction of Chartres Cathedral in France in the 13th century, a visitor was said to have approached two workers laying bricks. He first asked one of them, "What are you doing?" The man, tired and disheartened, responded, "I'm just laying bricks. It's hard, monotonous work, and it pays just enough to get by." His voice carried no enthusiasm, and his body language showed he felt burdened by his task.

The visitor then turned to the second worker and asked the same question. The man paused, smiled, and said, "I'm building a cathedral. This will be a magnificent place of worship, where people from all walks of life will gather to find peace, hope, and inspiration. It's an honor to be a part of something so grand and meaningful." His pride and enthusiasm were evident, and despite doing the same physical labor as the first man, he seemed to carry his task with a sense of purpose and joy.

This tale highlights the stark contrast in how the same work can be perceived, depending on whether one understands its greater significance. The worker who viewed his role as contributing to the creation of a cathedral felt a connection to the larger vision, which transformed a tedious task into a meaningful endeavor. It also speaks to the enduring importance of having a clear "why" in work, whether you're building a medieval cathedral or solving modern challenges.

Know thyself

"Know thyself" is an age-old adage emphasizing self-awareness's importance in personal growth, relationships, and career success. One tool that has gained widespread popularity in helping individuals understand themselves better is the Myers-Briggs Type Indicator (MBTI). Developed by Isabel Briggs Myers and Katharine Cook Briggs, the MBTI categorizes individuals into 16 distinct personality types based on their preferences in four dimensions:

Extraversion (E) vs. Introversion (I): How you gain energy—whether through external interactions or internal reflection.

Sensing (S) vs. Intuition (N): How you take in information—whether through concrete facts or abstract concepts.

Thinking (T) vs. Feeling (F): How you make decisions—whether based on logic or personal values.

Judging (J) vs. Perceiving (P): How you approach life—whether in a structured, planned way or a flexible, adaptable manner.

Why Knowing Yourself Through MBTI is Important:

Enhanced Self-Awareness:
The MBTI provides a structured framework to identify your strengths, weaknesses, and natural preferences. For example, an INTJ (Introverted, Intuitive, Thinking, Judging) might recognize their strengths in strategic planning and problem-solving but also understand their tendency to overlook emotional dynamics in a team.

Better Decision-Making:

Understanding your MBTI type helps you make career, lifestyle, and relationship choices that align with your inherent preferences. For instance, an ESFP (Extraverted, Sensing, Feeling, Perceiving) might thrive in dynamic environments with frequent social interaction, while an ISTP (Introverted, Sensing, Thinking, Perceiving) might excel in technical fields requiring hands-on problem-solving.

Improved Relationships:

The MBTI not only helps you understand yourself but also fosters empathy and effective communication with others. Knowing that your partner is an ENFP (Extraverted, Intuitive, Feeling, Perceiving) while you are an ISTJ (Introverted, Sensing, Thinking, Judging) can help you appreciate their spontaneity while addressing your need for structure.

Career Guidance:

MBTI insights can guide you toward roles that align with your natural abilities. For example, INFJs (Introverted, Intuitive, Feeling, Judging) often excel in counseling, writing, or roles requiring deep empathy, while ENTPs (Extraverted, Intuitive, Thinking, Perceiving) thrive in innovation-driven industries.

Conflict Resolution:

Self-awareness through MBTI equips you with the tools to navigate conflicts effectively. If you're a Thinker, you might learn to temper your logical approach with emotional sensitivity when dealing with a Feeler type, thus creating more harmonious interactions.

Personal Growth:

Recognizing your blind spots is critical for growth. An ENFJ (Extraverted, Intuitive, Feeling, Judging) might work on setting boundaries to avoid overcommitting, while an ISTP could strive to express their emotions more openly.

Imagine a workplace scenario where a team consists of individuals with varying MBTI types. The leader, an ENTJ, might focus on long-term goals and efficiency, while an ISFJ team member may emphasize team harmony and meeting everyone's needs. By understanding each other's MBTI preferences, the leader could adjust their approach to include more empathetic communication, while the team members might step out of their comfort zone to adopt a results-driven mindset when necessary.

The Myers-Briggs Personality Test is not just a label but a tool for self-reflection and growth. By understanding your MBTI type, you can navigate the complexities of life with clarity, leverage your strengths, address your limitations, and build deeper connections with those around you. In the journey of "knowing thyself," the MBTI offers a roadmap to uncovering your unique path. There are several other tests available for discovering your inner personality, including a test designed by Clifton for discovering your 5 core personality strengths. These tests will help you understand yourself better and therefore help you understand what you are good at naturally, and where your natural inclination is. After discovering the strengths and weaknesses we are ready to go through the final concept of this chapter IKIGAI.

Concept Of Ikigaia

The Japanese concept of Ikigai is a profound and holistic framework for finding fulfillment and purpose in one's life, particularly in the context of work. Translated roughly as "reason for being," Ikigai represents the sweet spot where four critical elements intersect: what you love, what you are good at, what the world needs, and what you can be paid for. Understanding and integrating these elements can provide a powerful roadmap to achieving lasting satisfaction and meaning in your professional life.

The Four Pillars of Ikigai

What You Love to Do (Passion):

This element reflects your intrinsic interests and joys—activities or pursuits that genuinely excite you. It's about discovering what makes your heart race and your spirit come alive. For instance, if you have a deep love for painting, this passion represents one part of your Ikigai.

What You Are Good At (Vocation):

This area encompasses your skills, talents, and competencies. It involves understanding what you excel at naturally or through acquired expertise. It's crucial to recognize your strengths and how they can be leveraged effectively. If you have a knack for problem-solving and analytical thinking, this is where your skill set aligns with your Ikigai.

What the World Needs (Mission):

This pillar focuses on the needs and problems of the world that you can address through your work. It's about contributing to society in a meaningful way. For example, if there is a growing need for sustainable environmental practices, and you have a passion for ecology, addressing this need aligns with the mission aspect of your Ikigai.

What You Can Be Paid For (Profession):

This component relates to finding a viable way to monetize your skills and passions. It's about ensuring that your work not only brings personal satisfaction but also provides financial stability. If you can turn your artistic talent into a successful career by selling your paintings or working in creative industries, you've touched on this aspect of Ikigai.

Discovering Your Ikigai: A Journey of Exploration

Finding your Ikigai is rarely a straightforward process; it often involves a journey of self-discovery and exploration. Here's how you might navigate this path:

Experimentation and Exploration:

To discover your Ikigai, you may need to engage in various experiences, roles, and projects. For example, you might try different job roles, volunteer in various capacities, or pursue side projects related to your interests. Each experience helps refine your understanding of what resonates with you.

Trial and Error:

It's essential to embrace the process of trial and error. Not every endeavor will lead to your Ikigai, and some paths may not work out as planned. However, each attempt provides valuable insights into what you enjoy and what doesn't align with your goals.

Reflection and Adaptation:

Regular reflection on your experiences is crucial. Consider keeping a journal to document what you enjoy, where you excel, and what you find fulfilling. Use this information to adapt and refine your pursuits, gradually honing in on your true calling.

Aligning Passions and Skills:

As you explore different paths, seek to align your passions with your skills. This alignment creates a sense of flow and fulfillment in your work. For instance, if you're passionate about writing and excel at it, exploring careers in writing, journalism, or content creation might bring you closer to your Ikigai.

Seeking Guidance:

Sometimes, seeking guidance from mentors, career coaches, or professionals in your field of interest can provide valuable perspectives. They can offer insights into how to align your passions and skills with real-world opportunities.

Continuous Adjustment:

Ikigai is not a static destination but a dynamic and evolving concept. As you grow and change, your understanding of Ikigai may shift. Be open to continuous adjustment and refinement of your path.

Conclusion

Work is more than just a means of earning a living; it's an integral part of our lives that affects our well-being, happiness, and overall life satisfaction. By embracing the power of elimination, focusing on creativity, and seeking to align with your Ikigai, you can turn work from a source of stress into a fulfilling, rewarding aspect of your life.

CHAPTER SIX

TIME

Time is the most valuable resource we have. Unlike money, which can be earned, saved, or invested, time moves forward relentlessly, and once spent, it can never be recovered. Yet, in today's fast-paced world, we often treat time as though it is infinite, placing more value on material wealth, status, and productivity. Time affluence, a concept that many overlook, is the feeling of having enough time to pursue activities that bring joy, fulfillment, and relaxation. In this chapter, we explore the importance of time affluence, why it is so often undervalued, and how to cultivate a life that prioritizes time over money.

The concept of dimensions helps us understand the framework of the universe, both in terms of space and time. Let's explore the three dimensions of space and the three dimensions of time (past, present, and future) while understanding why we can traverse spatial dimensions freely but not temporal ones.

Three Dimensions of Space

Space is described using three dimensions that define the physical placement of objects in the universe:

Length (X-axis):

This dimension represents horizontal measurements. For example, the width of a room or the distance between two cities.

Width (Y-axis):

This represents vertical measurements, such as the height of a building or a mountain.

Depth (Z-axis):

Depth adds the perception of distance into or out of a plane. It helps create a three-dimensional view, such as the depth of a pool or how far an object is from you.

These three dimensions work together to define the position of any object in space. For example, the position of a chair in a room is determined by its distance along these three axes.

Three Dimensions of Time

Time, unlike space, is linear and has three conceptual dimensions:

Past:

Events that have already occurred. The past provides lessons and context but is fixed and unchangeable.

Present:

The fleeting moment where actions and decisions happen. It's the only dimension of time where you can actively make changes.

Future:

Events that are yet to occur. The future holds possibilities but remains uncertain until the present shapes it.

Why Can We Traverse Through Space but Not Time?

Traversal Through Space:

Humans can move freely in all three spatial dimensions. For instance, you can walk forward and backward (length), move side to side (width), or jump up and down (height).

This freedom is due to the physical properties of space and our ability to physically act within it.

Why Time is Different:

Time's Unidirectional Flow (Arrow of Time):

Time moves forward in a linear fashion due to the Second Law of Thermodynamics, which states that entropy (disorder) increases over time. This creates a "time arrow" pointing from past to future. Unlike space, time doesn't allow for backtracking or halting.

Fixed Nature of the Past:

While we can recall and learn from the past, it is immutable. The past is "recorded," much like a book that's already been written.

Uncertainty of the Future:

The future doesn't exist yet; it's shaped by actions in the present. Unlike spatial movement, which is determined by clear coordinates, movement into the future remains speculative.

Relativity of Time:

According to Einstein's theory of relativity, time behaves differently based on the observer's motion and gravitational field. While it's theoretically possible to manipulate the perception of time (e.g., time dilation), actual travel to the past or future in the same way we navigate space isn't possible.

How We "Traverse" Time Mentally

Although we can't physically move through time:

In the Past: We revisit memories, analyze past events, and learn lessons.

In the Future: We use imagination and planning to project possibilities.

In the Present: We act, creating a bridge between the past and future.

This mental "traversal" influences how we interact with space and our decisions.

Analogy: Space vs. Time Traversal

Imagine a movie:

The screen (spatial dimensions) allows you to see the entire movie frame at once. You can pause, rewind, or fast-forward.

The play button (time) dictates the sequence of events. You can't skip to the future or return to the past in real life as you would with a movie.

While space offers the freedom to move in any direction, time is a one-way journey governed by physical laws. Understanding this distinction highlights the importance of living fully in the present, learning from the past, and planning wisely for the future while grounded in the three dimensions of space.

Concept of Time Affluence

Dr. Laurie Santos, a professor at Yale University, offers profound insights into happiness and well-being in her widely acclaimed course "The Science of Well-Being." One of the central themes of her course is that our minds are not particularly good at predicting what will bring us true happiness. We often believe that achieving wealth, gaining social status, or acquiring material possessions—like a big house, a fancy car, or the latest gadgets—will lead to happiness. Yet, research shows that the pursuit of these things frequently results in the opposite: more stress, frustration, and dissatisfaction.

Instead of focusing on material gain, Dr. Santos presents a list of eight scientifically proven factors that enhance well-being, and surprisingly, money doesn't make the cut. The eight factors she highlights are:

Acts of Kindness: Engaging in kind acts toward others fosters a sense of connection, purpose, and positivity.

Exercise: Physical activity is consistently linked to improved mood and reduced stress levels.

Social Connection: Meaningful relationships with friends, family, and community significantly contribute to happiness.

Meditation: Mindfulness practices can help reduce anxiety, enhance focus, and promote emotional well-being.

Time Affluence: Having the feeling of control over your own time and not being rushed or over-scheduled.

Good Sleep: Sleep is vital for cognitive function, emotional balance, and overall health.

Gratitude: Practicing gratitude shifts focus from what is lacking to appreciating what we have, boosting happiness and contentment.

Goal-Setting: Setting and pursuing meaningful goals provides direction and fulfillment.

While all of these factors contribute to well-being, time affluence stands out as particularly crucial, yet it's often overlooked. Time affluence is the perception that you have enough time to do the things that matter to you, and it contrasts sharply with the cultural emphasis on productivity and financial success.

The Overlooked Value of Time Affluence

In today's fast-paced world, time affluence is often sacrificed in the relentless pursuit of career advancement, productivity, and material wealth. People willingly exchange their time for higher salaries, promotions, and the luxuries of modern life. Yet, studies show that this trade-off doesn't necessarily lead to happiness. We are conditioned to believe that success and wealth will make us happy, but the reality is more complicated.

The issue is that time, unlike money, is a non-renewable resource. Once spent, it's gone forever. Despite this, we often prioritize accumulating more wealth over protecting our free time. We may say, "I'll work hard now so I can enjoy life later," but this mentality can lead to burnout and missed opportunities for joy in the present. While money can buy comfort and convenience, it cannot buy time—something that becomes painfully clear when people reflect on their lives.

A World Obsessed with Productivity

In our society, productivity is often celebrated and equated with worth. People push themselves to the limit with busy schedules, filling every minute with tasks, meetings, or work-related activities. In this productivity-centric culture, time affluence is rarely prioritized. However, the stress and overwhelm from constant busyness can take a toll on mental health and relationships. People often find themselves longing for more free time, even as they accumulate more wealth or success.

The psychological cost of this imbalance is substantial. Lack of time leads to feelings of helplessness, frustration, and dissatisfaction. We may start to feel disconnected from loved ones, disengaged from activities we once enjoyed, and distanced from our own sense of well-being.

Shifting the Focus: Time Over Money

Santos' research suggests that instead of chasing more money, status, or material possessions, we would be better off seeking more time—time for the things that truly matter, like spending quality moments with loved ones, engaging in hobbies, and resting. Time affluence offers a sense of freedom and control that is far more valuable than material wealth.

This doesn't mean that financial success isn't important, but rather that we should balance our pursuit of wealth with a conscious effort to protect our time. Allocating time for self-care, meaningful relationships, relaxation, and hobbies can create a greater sense of happiness and fulfillment than working long hours in the hope of financial gain. As the saying goes, "Time is money," but a more accurate interpretation might be that time is more valuable than money.

Time vs. Money: A Tradeoff

Imagine for a moment that a billionaire offers to exchange all of their wealth for a portion of your remaining lifespan. Would you accept that deal? Most people would instantly refuse because they recognize that time is priceless. It brings with it opportunities for experiences, growth, and the chance to live life on our own terms. Despite this, many of us unknowingly trade away our time every day for something far less valuable: money. And ironically, money isn't even on the list of Dr. Laurie Santos' happiness factors. So why do we do it? Because we've been conditioned to believe that material success equals happiness.

From a young age, society teaches us that the path to happiness lies in achieving wealth. We work long hours, sacrificing time with loved ones or personal pursuits, all in the name of higher salaries, larger homes, and a collection of material goods. The irony is that these very things—money, status, possessions—rarely bring the deep fulfillment we're seeking. Instead, they often come at the cost of time, which we could have spent doing the things that genuinely bring joy and meaning.

The Necessary Pursuit of Money

Of course, the pursuit of money isn't inherently wrong or avoidable. For many, it's a necessary means to survive and meet basic needs such as food, shelter, healthcare, and security. Without money, life becomes uncertain and stressful. Yet, there's a tipping point—a moment when the accumulation of wealth shifts from fulfilling basic needs to chasing after desires, competition, and status. This shift can be dangerous because it changes the way we view the relationship between time and money.

When our needs transition into wants, we start trading even more of our time for money. We work harder, taking on more projects, more hours, and more responsibilities, all to afford luxuries that, in many cases, we don't even have time to enjoy. We end up in a vicious cycle, where more money seems to demand more time, leaving us with less space for what truly matters in life.

The Paradox of Time and Money

The paradox here is both profound and unsettling: While we're constantly striving to earn more money to live a better life, we often sacrifice the very time that makes life worth living. We fall into the trap of thinking that if we just had more money, we'd have the freedom to do what we love. Yet, in reality, the more we chase after wealth, the less time we have to spend on the activities and relationships that bring true happiness. In contrast, those who have reached financial stability often start to realize the true value of time. The wealthy, once they attain a certain level of financial security, frequently begin to use their money to buy back their time. They outsource chores, hire help for mundane tasks, and invest in passive income streams. Their goal shifts from accumulating wealth to gaining freedom—freedom from time-consuming tasks, freedom to explore hobbies, or even just the freedom to rest. The ultimate aim becomes not more money, but more time to live life meaningfully.

Money as a Tool

At its core, money is nothing more than a tool. It's a means to an end, but not the end itself. The critical question is: What is the true goal? For many, the answer should be freedom—the freedom to live life according to personal values, the freedom to spend time in ways that are meaningful, fulfilling, and joyous. When we see money as a tool, rather than the final destination, we can start to reshape how we prioritize it in our lives. Instead of constantly chasing after more, we can seek to create balance—to ensure that we're spending time, our most precious resource, on things that align with our values and aspirations. Time, unlike money, can never be replenished, and that makes it the one commodity we must guard most carefully.

In the end, it's essential to remind ourselves that while money can provide comfort and security, it cannot replace time. Time is what makes life rich, and allows us to connect with loved ones, pursue passions, and simply enjoy the present moment. When we stop trading too much of our time for the pursuit of wealth and status, we unlock the possibility of a life that is both rich and fulfilling in the ways that truly matter.

The Illusion of Early Retirement

The concept of early retirement has surged in popularity in recent years, with the rise of financial influencers, or "fin-fluencers," who advocate for financial independence and the idea of retiring in your 40s or 50s. The appeal is obvious: imagine trading the daily grind for a life of leisure, travel, hobbies, and passion projects long before the traditional retirement age. But behind the enticing allure of early retirement lies a series of challenges and misconceptions that often go unaddressed.

The Dream vs. Reality

On the surface, early retirement seems like the ultimate goal. Who wouldn't want to stop working while still young enough to enjoy life fully? Financial independence, the idea of living off investments and savings, promises a life free of the 9-to-5, where you can spend your time exactly as you wish. However, this vision often romanticizes early retirement without accounting for its complexities.

One of the most significant misconceptions is that once you reach early retirement, all problems will disappear, and life will automatically be more fulfilling. The reality is often far more nuanced. While the freedom to stop working is attractive, many people underestimate the psychological and emotional implications of stepping away from a structured work life at an early age.

Changing Needs and Financial Challenges

One of the most common pitfalls of early retirement is underestimating financial needs. While people save aggressively to achieve this goal, many don't account for the fact that lifestyle needs to change over time. What seems like an adequate amount of savings at 40 may not stretch far enough when healthcare costs rise, inflation accelerates, or unexpected expenses emerge. Additionally, people often fail to account for the fact that retirement is long—potentially lasting 30 or 40 years. The cost of living increases, market fluctuations occur, and personal circumstances change. These unpredictable factors can lead to financial strain for those who thought they had more than enough to last. When you retire early, you're betting on the fact that you can sustain yourself financially for the remainder of your life, but unforeseen circumstances—from medical issues to economic downturns—can quickly erode your nest egg.

The Loss of Purpose

Beyond the financial challenges, early retirees often face something even more daunting: the loss of purpose. Work provides more than just a paycheck; it gives us structure, routine, a sense of accomplishment, and, often, social connections. Many people find fulfillment in their careers, or at least in the sense of contribution and achievement that work provides.

Without the responsibilities and goals that come with a job, early retirees may feel adrift. The early days of retirement might feel like a vacation—filled with travel, relaxation, and hobbies—but as time goes on, the lack of a clear purpose can lead to feelings of boredom or even depression. Finding meaningful activities to replace the role work once played is crucial, yet many people fail to consider this challenge when chasing the early retirement dream.

The Uncertainty of the Future

The world is unpredictable, and despite our best efforts to plan, life has a way of throwing curveballs. Major events like the global financial crisis in 2008, the COVID-19 pandemic, and other black swan events have demonstrated that no matter how carefully we save or invest, the future is uncertain. Economic shifts, job market changes, or personal crises can quickly alter even the most well-laid retirement plans.

For example, during the COVID-19 pandemic, many early retirees saw their investment portfolios take a hit, forcing them to reconsider their financial situation. The sudden shift in the economy meant that what once seemed like a secure financial future could suddenly look very different. The risk is that once you've retired early, you may not have the flexibility to return to work if needed, especially in a rapidly changing job market.

The Shifting Goalposts

For those aiming for early retirement, the goalpost is often in motion. What was once enough savings might no longer feel sufficient as unforeseen expenses arise or market conditions change. As a result, many find themselves having to adjust their plans—saving more, working longer, or reconsidering retirement altogether.

Additionally, as life progresses, people's desires and ambitions often shift. What seems like the perfect retirement plan in your 30s may no longer align with your values or lifestyle in your 50s. Life is full of changes, and the flexibility to adapt is key to long-term happiness and security.

Time Budgeting: A New Approach to Life

In today's fast-paced world, it's easy to get swept up in the rush of productivity goals, the allure of early retirement, and the pursuit of a work-life balance that seems increasingly elusive. However, rather than fixating solely on financial freedom or early retirement, there's a more immediate, practical solution that can transform the way we live: time budgeting. Just as we carefully manage our money with financial budgets, time budgeting allows us to manage our most valuable resource—time—with purpose and precision.

The Great Equalizer

Unlike money, which is distributed unequally, time is the one resource that every person has in equal measure. Whether you're the president of a country, a CEO of a major corporation, or an everyday worker, you have the same 24 hours in a day. The key difference between success and stagnation often lies in how those 24 hours are spent.

Take, for instance, how high-powered leaders and successful entrepreneurs budget their time. Their calendars are not left to chance—they meticulously schedule every hour to align with their priorities. Important tasks are tackled during their peak hours, usually in the morning when their energy and focus are at their highest. Less important tasks are left for times when they're mentally fatigued or distracted, ensuring that the best hours of the day are spent on work that truly matters. This approach is deliberate and strategic, designed to optimize productivity and focus on the most important goals.

Time Wasted is Time Lost

But time budgeting is not just for CEOs or high-powered executives. It's a concept that everyone can benefit from. How many times have you found yourself sitting in a meeting, wondering if it could have been an email instead? Or scrolling through social media, wasting hours on trivial tasks that add no real value to your personal or professional life? Meetings, in particular, are notorious for being time sinks. Studies show that the average employee spends over six hours a day in meetings—many of which are deemed unnecessary or unproductive. Jason Fried and David Heinemeier Hansson, authors of Rework, argue that time wasted in meetings is time stolen from more meaningful work.

This resonates with many who feel that a significant portion of their workday is lost to activities that don't truly matter.

Aligning Time with Priorities

Time budgeting requires us to take a closer look at where our hours are going and how we can better align them with our priorities. It's not just about fitting more into your day—it's about fitting the right things into your day. Much like financial budgeting, where you allocate funds to essential categories like housing, food, and savings, time budgeting involves allocating hours to the most important aspects of your life. This could be work, but it could also be time for exercise, personal growth, or family.

Instead of letting the day run you, time budgeting puts you back in control. For instance, if your mornings are your most productive time, schedule your most challenging tasks during those hours. This could mean focusing on deep work—projects that require creativity and focus—early in the day. Conversely, you might save routine, less mentally demanding tasks, like responding to emails, for the afternoon when your energy wanes.

Avoiding the Trivial Many

A key component of time budgeting is understanding what tasks and activities are truly valuable versus what tasks are simply time-fillers. The Pareto Principle, or the 80/20 rule, suggests that 80% of results come from 20% of efforts. In the context of time budgeting, this means that the most important and impactful work often comes from just a small fraction of your day. The challenge is identifying and prioritizing that 20% while eliminating or minimizing the less important tasks.

For example, you might notice that you spend hours each week attending meetings that don't contribute to your main objectives. A time audit could reveal these inefficiencies and lead you to ask for fewer meetings, set stricter agendas, or request that updates be handled via email or collaborative tools instead. The aim is to guard your time fiercely, using it for activities that move the needle toward your long-term goals.

Time as the Ultimate Resource

Time budgeting is about more than just becoming more productive. It's about living with intention. As much as we might want to increase our earnings, build wealth, and achieve financial security, no amount of money can buy back lost time. This is why time budgeting is essential—it forces us to become aware of how we're spending our time and helps us make more conscious decisions.

By prioritizing your time, you gain the freedom to focus on what matters most, whether that's work, relationships, or personal passions. It's the antidote to feeling overwhelmed, overcommitted, and constantly busy without real purpose. When you budget your time effectively, you not only accomplish more but also feel more fulfilled, knowing that your hours are spent on activities that align with your values.

Consider asking yourself these questions:

What would you do if you had more free time?

How would you spend your days if money weren't a factor?

These questions can help you clarify your values and understand what truly matters to you. The answers will guide you toward a life where time is abundant and spent on things that bring genuine joy and fulfillment.

Prioritizing Experiences, Relationships, and Growth

Time affluence also involves a shift in prioritizing experiences over things. While material possessions may bring short-term pleasure, it's the experiences, relationships, and personal growth that create long-lasting happiness. Research consistently shows that people who prioritize experiences—whether it's a trip with friends, learning a new skill, or spending quality time with family—report higher levels of satisfaction and well-being.

Building stronger relationships is a cornerstone of time affluence. When you create time for your loved ones, you're investing in bonds that bring emotional richness to your life. Imagine spending an uninterrupted evening with your partner, fully present in conversation, or playing with your children without thinking about the next day's deadlines. These are the moments that make life fulfilling, not the latest gadget or designer item.

Additionally, personal growth is often sacrificed in the pursuit of material success. With time affluence, you can reclaim time to focus on self-improvement and growth—whether that means reading, learning new skills, practicing mindfulness, or even just taking time to reflect and recalibrate. When you prioritize your personal development, you not only enrich your own life but also create a ripple effect that positively impacts those around you.

Reimagining Success

In a world driven by productivity and financial success, time affluence asks us to reimagine success. Instead of measuring it by how much money we make or how many hours we work, success becomes about how much freedom we have to spend our time on the things we love. It's about waking up each day with the ability to choose how we want to live, rather than feeling dictated by obligations and societal expectations.

Ultimately, time affluence isn't just about having free time—it's about having control over your time and the ability to direct it toward what matters most to you. By embracing this mindset, you can step off the treadmill of constant accumulation and begin to live a life that is truly rich—not in material wealth, but in experiences, relationships, and personal satisfaction.

Why Timing Matters in Strategy Execution

Timing is a critical factor in the successful execution of any strategy. Each step in a plan serves a specific purpose and builds upon the previous one. If the sequence is disrupted, such as executing step 15 on day 1, the foundational work required for that step's success is often missing. This lack of preparation, context, or resources can lead to failure, regardless of how well the step is designed.

Foundation Building:
Each step lays the groundwork for the next. For example, step 15 might depend on the outcomes of steps 1–14, such as gathering data, building resources, or establishing relationships. Skipping foundational steps can

leave critical gaps that undermine the entire strategy.

Readiness:
Timing ensures that you and your team are prepared to handle the challenges of each phase. If step 15 requires advanced skills or knowledge developed in earlier steps, jumping ahead will likely lead to confusion, inefficiency, and poor outcomes.

Resource Alignment:
Strategies often require resources—be it time, finances, or personnel—allocated in stages. Attempting a later step prematurely may result in resource shortages or mismanagement.

Stakeholder Involvement:
Many strategies involve collaboration with stakeholders. These relationships take time to nurture and prematurely introducing complex steps may alienate key partners or create resistance.

Learning and Adaptation:
Each step provides valuable insights that inform the subsequent ones. Skipping steps means missing out on learning opportunities, which could lead to repeated mistakes or misaligned goals.

Risk Management:
A step-by-step approach allows you to identify and mitigate risks gradually. Jumping ahead increases exposure to unforeseen challenges that could derail the strategy entirely.

Example:
   Imagine you're building a business, and step 15 is "Scaling Operations," while step 1 is "Identifying Market Needs." If you attempt to scale operations without first understanding your market, you might produce goods or services no one wants. The resources spent on scaling would be wasted, and the business would likely face financial strain or collapse.

Alternatively, consider a fitness journey where step 15 involves advanced strength training, but steps 1–14 involve building foundational fitness and proper form. Starting with step 15 could lead to injuries or burnout because your body isn't ready for the intensity.

Executing a strategy is like constructing a building—you can't start with the roof before laying the foundation. Each step is carefully placed in sequence to maximize the chances of success. Skipping ahead may seem like a shortcut, but it often leads to setbacks, inefficiencies, or outright failure. Trust the process, respect the timing, and focus on completing one step at a time to build a strong, sustainable outcome.

The Story of Tom: From Busywork to Following His Passion

Tom was a software engineer at a large tech company, and to anyone who worked with him, he seemed like the perfect employee—always busy, always working. Tom would stay late at the office, respond to emails immediately, and attend every meeting, even when his input wasn't needed. He was known for his hustle and tireless work ethic, but deep down, Tom wasn't happy. Despite always looking busy, he felt like his days were filled with meaningless tasks that didn't really move the needle.

Tom had a passion outside of work that he had been neglecting for years—painting. Before he got wrapped up in the corporate world, Tom had spent hours each week in his small home studio, painting landscapes and experimenting with colors. But with his long work hours and constant pressure to stay busy, he had convinced himself that there was no time left for his art.

One evening, after yet another long day filled with trivial tasks and back-to-back meetings, Tom had a realization: being busy wasn't making him happy, and it certainly wasn't getting him closer to his real passion. He decided to make a change. Tom knew that he couldn't continue wasting time on things that didn't matter just to feel productive. He needed to eliminate the unimportant to make room for what truly mattered to him.

The first thing Tom did was assess how he spent his time at work. He quickly realized that many of his tasks were low-priority—responding to emails immediately, attending meetings that didn't require his presence, and doing small, routine tasks that could easily be delegated or automated.

Tom started by cutting down on unnecessary meetings and setting boundaries for checking his email only twice a day. He also learned to delegate some of the routine tasks to junior team members, which not only freed up his time but also helped his colleagues grow.

With his newfound free time, Tom set a firm goal: he would spend an hour every evening painting, no matter what. At first, it was hard to shake off the habit of filling every minute with work, but as he gradually adjusted to his new routine, he started to feel more fulfilled. That one hour of painting each evening gave him a sense of peace and purpose that his busy work had never provided. He also rediscovered the joy he felt when creating art, something that had been missing from his life for far too long.

As the weeks went by, Tom found himself thriving both personally and professionally. By eliminating the trivial tasks that made him look busy but didn't contribute to his growth, he not only reclaimed time for his passion but also became more focused and effective at work. He started taking on higher-value projects that actually excited him, and his productivity improved. In fact, his manager noticed the difference and praised him for his newfound efficiency and creativity.

With his evenings dedicated to painting, Tom's passion project began to grow. He started sharing his artwork online, and to his surprise, people loved it. What had once been a neglected hobby was now a thriving part of his life. Tom even began selling some of his paintings and was invited to showcase his work at a local gallery. He felt more alive and fulfilled than he had in years.

Tom's story shows the power of eliminating trivial tasks and replacing them with time spent on what truly matters. By letting go of the need to look busy, Tom was able to follow his passion for painting and rediscover a part of himself he thought he had lost. In the process, he found a balance between work and his personal life that left him happier, more productive, and more fulfilled.

How Timing Influences the Outcome:

Timing plays a crucial role in shaping the experience and perceived value of any accomplishment. When tasks or goals are not achieved within their intended timeframe, the significance and satisfaction derived from them often diminish. This delay can affect personal growth, professional opportunities, and even the emotional resonance of the achievement.

Relevance Diminishes Over Time:

Completing a task too late might render it irrelevant. For example, delivering a critical project after the deadline in a competitive industry might mean losing a client, even if the quality of the work is excellent. The context of the task's completion matters as much as the task itself.

Emotional Impact Reduces:

Achieving a goal at the right time brings a sense of fulfillment and joy. For instance, graduating on schedule is a proud milestone celebrated with peers. Graduating late, though still an accomplishment, might feel less exciting as the original moment of celebration has passed.

Opportunities Can Be Missed:

Success often hinges on aligning with the right opportunity. A musician who releases a song years after a trend has passed may struggle to connect with an audience, even if the song is good. Being timely means leveraging the momentum of existing opportunities.

Effort vs. Reward Imbalance:

If a task is delayed, the effort required to complete it might increase while the reward diminishes. For example, resolving a conflict late may demand more energy and compromise than if it had been addressed immediately, often yielding a less satisfying resolution.

Lessons Delayed are Lessons Lost:

Timely accomplishments often serve as stepping stones for future goals. If delayed, they may impede progress, causing stagnation. For instance, mastering a skill at the right stage of your career can open doors to new roles. Learning it too late might mean missing those opportunities altogether.

Example: *Missing the Timing of a Task*

Imagine planting a garden. If seeds are sown in the correct season, they flourish and yield fruits or flowers. If planted late, the seeds may still sprout but might face harsher conditions, reduced growth, or complete failure. The experience of reaping the benefits changes drastically based on timing. Similarly, achieving professional or personal milestones after the optimal moment may feel more like catching up than celebrating success.

Why Timeliness Matters:

Creates Momentum:

Accomplishing tasks on time builds confidence and sets the pace for future goals. It fosters a sense of control and alignment with the bigger picture.

Maximizes Impact:

Timely actions allow you to make the most of favorable circumstances, ensuring that the effort translates into meaningful results.

Preserves Motivation:

Delays often lead to diminished enthusiasm. Achieving on-time reinforces motivation and encourages consistent effort.

Timely execution of tasks is not just about checking off items on a list; it's about maximizing the value, experience, and impact of the accomplishment. Aligning actions with the right time amplifies their significance and creates a sense of flow that propels progress. Conversely, delays can dilute the value, making even hard-earned success feel underwhelming.

Why Timing is Critical

Timing is often the make-or-break factor in the success of any venture, particularly for startups. Even with a great product or innovative idea, entering the market at the wrong time can lead to failure, while startups that launch at the right moment often thrive. Timing determines whether a business can align with market demand, customer readiness, and the availability of complementary technologies or infrastructure.

Market Readiness:

A startup that launches before the market is ready may struggle to find customers or face resistance to adopting a new idea. Conversely, entering too late means facing intense competition or a saturated market.

Consumer Behavior Trends:

Timing must align with shifts in consumer preferences. If a startup launches a product that matches current trends or anticipates future ones, it can capture the market's attention and gain momentum.

Technological Support:

Many startups depend on supporting technologies. If the infrastructure, tools, or devices needed for their product or service are not yet widely available, their growth will be stunted.

Economic Environment:

The state of the economy can affect whether people or businesses are willing to invest in or adopt new products. Startups launching during economic booms may see higher adoption rates, while those launching in recessions might struggle.

Competitive Landscape:

Entering a market too early can mean educating customers at high costs, while entering too late may mean facing well-established competitors.

Examples of Timing in Startup Success and Failure:

Success Stories:

Airbnb:
Airbnb launched during the 2008 financial crisis, a time when many people were looking for affordable travel options or ways to supplement their income by renting out space. The economic downturn created a perfect market condition for Airbnb to thrive.

Zoom:
While Zoom existed before the COVID-19 pandemic, its timing in scaling its operations and marketing made it the go-to platform for remote work and communication when the pandemic hit. The external circumstance of global lockdowns accelerated its adoption.

Failure Stories:

Webvan:
An online grocery delivery service in the late 1990s, Webvan failed because it was ahead of its time. The technology, infrastructure, and consumer readiness for online grocery shopping were not developed enough, leading to its collapse.

Friendster:
Friendster, a pioneer in social networking, launched before people were fully ready to adopt the concept of sharing personal information online. It struggled with technical issues and was ultimately overtaken by Facebook, which entered the market later when users were more familiar with social media.

Lessons from Timing

Research Market Readiness:
Startups should assess whether their target audience is ready to adopt the product or service. Early adopters can help create a buzz, but the mainstream market must follow for sustained success.

Stay Aware of Trends and Technologies:
Keep an eye on emerging trends, shifts in consumer behavior, and advancements in technology to time your launch effectively.

Adapt to External Circumstances:
Flexibility is key. If the timing isn't right, startups should pivot their strategies or delay launches rather than pushing forward prematurely.

Learn from Competitors:
Analyze why previous startups in your industry succeeded or failed to understand how timing influenced their outcomes.

Startups that align their timing with market readiness, technological infrastructure, and economic conditions can achieve exponential growth. However, mistiming—whether launching too early or too late—can result in wasted resources, missed opportunities, or outright failure. Strategic timing isn't about luck; it's about understanding the pulse of the market and adapting your execution accordingly.

Conclusion

Time affluence is the ultimate form of wealth. It's the freedom to live life on your own terms, without the constant pressure to trade your time for money. While financial security is important, it's not the key to happiness. Instead, happiness comes from how we choose to spend our time — on meaningful activities, with people we care about, and in ways that nourish our souls. By Eliminating unnecessary activities from our day-to-day lives, we can create a life that is not only productive but also deeply fulfilling.

CHAPTER SEVEN

ANYTHING IN EXCESS

अतिरूपेण वै सीता चातिगर्वेण रावणः। अतिदानाद् बलिर्बद्धो ह्यति सर्वत्र वर्जयेत्।।

This ancient Sanskrit verse from Chanakya Neeti translates to:

Sita, due to her extreme beauty, was kidnapped by Ravana. Ravana, due to his extreme arrogance, was killed in battle. King Bali, due to his extreme generosity, was tricked and lost everything. Thus, excess in anything is to be avoided.

The wisdom in this verse is timeless, teaching us that anything in excess, even virtues, can lead to downfall. It captures the essence of the dangers that lurk when things exceed their natural balance, be it beauty, pride, or generosity. In life, extremes are often seductive — they can appear as the pinnacle of success or the height of virtue — but they can also be the very things that unravel us.

The Tale of Excess in Ramayana

The first example in the verse is of Sita, the heroine of the epic Ramayana. Her beauty, often described as divine, was one of the reasons for her abduction by Ravana, the king of Lanka. Ravana, in his excessive pride and desire, could not see the consequences of his actions. His attraction to Sita's unmatched beauty blinded him to the moral and ethical boundaries he crossed, leading ultimately to his destruction.

This teaches us that even qualities we consider positive, like beauty or talent, can lead to harm when taken to an extreme. Sita's beauty became both a blessing and a curse. Ravana's desire for something as transient as physical beauty caused the ruin of an entire kingdom.

In life, we often admire those who possess extreme qualities — be it beauty, intelligence, or strength — without considering the potential consequences. A balance must be struck, for excess can breed greed, envy, and eventually destruction.

Ravana's Arrogance and Downfall

Ravana, the second character mentioned in the verse, is a powerful king who is also a symbol of excessive ego and arrogance. He was a great scholar and warrior, but his downfall was his inability to balance his strengths with humility. Ravana believed that his powers made him invincible, and this hubris led him to commit the heinous act of abducting Sita, thinking he could outwit destiny and defy Lord Rama.

His arrogance blinded him to his vulnerabilities, and he paid the ultimate price with his life. Ravana's story is a cautionary tale of how excess pride can lead to one's ruin. When we let our egos grow unchecked, we become incapable of seeing our own flaws, making us more prone to making destructive decisions.

In today's world, we see similar instances of downfall caused by unchecked pride. Leaders, entrepreneurs, and even ordinary people who let their ego dictate their actions often find themselves facing failure and isolation. Pride, when taken to an extreme, distorts judgment, making it difficult to distinguish between right and wrong.

The Generosity of King Bali

The final figure mentioned in the verse is King Bali, a character from the Puranic stories. King Bali was known for his extreme generosity, a virtue praised by all. However, even his goodness led to his downfall. When the god Vishnu, in the form of Vamana, asked Bali for land equivalent to three paces, the overly generous king agreed without hesitation. Vamana then expanded to cover the entire universe in two steps, leaving no space for the third step. Bali, true to his word, offered his head for the final step and lost everything, including his kingdom, to fulfill his promise.

Bali's excessive generosity teaches us that even good deeds, when performed in excess without proper consideration, can be harmful. Generosity, a quality often celebrated, becomes dangerous when it is boundless, as it opens us up to exploitation and self-destruction. While giving is important, it is equally important to set boundaries and maintain a balance between helping others and ensuring one's own well-being.

In modern times, excessive generosity can manifest in different forms, such as saying "yes" to every request, overextending oneself in relationships, or giving away more than one can afford. Without healthy limits, generosity can drain our energy, finances, and emotional resources, depleting us.

The Christian Perspective: The Seven Deadly Sins

The Christian perspective on excess, particularly through the lens of the Seven Deadly Sins, offers timeless lessons about the dangers of unchecked desires.

These sins—pride, greed, lust, envy, gluttony, wrath, and sloth

are warnings against the human tendency to overindulge in various aspects of life, leading to personal and societal harm. Among them, gluttony is particularly relevant to our modern world, as it extends beyond mere overconsumption of food to include any form of excessive indulgence, whether it's wealth, power, or even attention.

Gluttony reminds us that overindulgence, in any form, comes with consequences. In the pursuit of more—more food, more money, more recognition—we often consume far beyond what we need, draining resources that could be shared with others. This behavior leads not only to inequality but also to a depletion of moral and spiritual well-being. It fosters selfishness, entitlement, and disconnection from the values of community and compassion.

For instance, in today's consumer-driven society, we are constantly bombarded with messages that encourage overconsumption. Advertisements entice us to buy bigger houses, faster cars, and the latest gadgets. Social media feeds fuel a culture of comparison, urging us to chase the lifestyles of the rich and famous. However, this relentless pursuit of "more" often comes at a high cost. Excessive consumption, driven by gluttony, depletes natural resources, harms the environment, and takes a toll on both physical and mental health.

The Seven Deadly Sins, and particularly the warnings against gluttony, offer a vital reminder to seek balance. Instead of indulging in excess, Christianity encourages us to practice moderation, contentment, and gratitude. This approach to life fosters a deeper sense of fulfillment, as it shifts the focus from selfish accumulation to a more sustainable, meaningful existence.

In today's world, where excess is often celebrated and moderation is undervalued, the teachings of the Seven Deadly Sins provide a moral compass. By curbing our desires and embracing restraint, we can lead lives that are not only more balanced but also more righteous and fulfilling, allowing us to make meaningful contributions to the well-being of others and the world around us.

The Story of Shul Kumar: When Wealth Becomes Excess

A modern example of how excess can lead to downfall is the story of Shul Kumar, a man who won 5 crore rupees (around $670,000) on the Indian version of Who Wants to Be a Millionaire, known as Kaun Banega Crorepati. After winning the grand prize, Kumar's life changed dramatically — but not for the better. In a short span of time, he lost all of his winnings and went bankrupt, forced to return to a regular job to make ends meet.

The story of Shul Kumar serves as a poignant example of how sudden wealth can bring about unforeseen challenges and, in many cases, more harm than good. Kumar, an unassuming man from a modest background, skyrocketed to fame when he won 5 crore rupees on Kaun Banega Crorepati. In an instant, his life changed. What had once been a simple existence was now filled with the trappings of wealth and fame. But as quickly as the money came, it began to slip away.

At first, Kumar's heart was in the right place. He wanted to use his newfound fortune to help others. Family members, friends, and even strangers reached out to him, seeking financial aid, loans, and business investments. He found it difficult to say no, feeling an obligation to share his good fortune with those around him. However, this generosity, though well-intentioned, quickly spiraled out of control. Instead of setting boundaries or seeking financial advice, Kumar allowed himself to be overwhelmed by the demands of others.

Without proper financial planning or investment strategies, his wealth rapidly dwindled. Temptations and pressures mounted as he was pulled in multiple directions. People who he thought had his best interests at heart were often just seeking a piece of the pie. Kumar, in his excitement, lost sight of the need for financial discipline and long-term thinking. He didn't invest or save in ways that could secure his future. Instead, his winnings were spent or distributed with little regard for sustainability.

The weight of expectations, the demands from others, and the fast-paced lifestyle that came with wealth were a far cry from the life he once knew. What should have been a story of success and security became one of stress, anxiety, and, ultimately, failure. In the end, he was forced to return to a regular job to make ends meet, having lost all of his winnings.

Shul Kumar's story echoes the ancient cautionary tales from mythology, where excess often leads to downfall. Like King Ravana's pride or King Bali's unchecked generosity, Kumar's inability to manage the overwhelming forces around him led to his undoing. It highlights a vital truth: wealth, when not handled with care, can become more of a curse than a blessing.

The Dangers of Excess in Modern Life

In today's world, excess manifests in countless ways. We live in a time of information overload, where we are bombarded with data, news, and opinions every second. The constant stream of information can create confusion and anxiety, making it difficult to think clearly or make sound decisions.

The excess of consumerism is another example. We are encouraged to buy more, own more, and consume more than we need, leading to financial stress, environmental degradation, and social inequality. The pursuit of material excess often leaves us feeling empty and dissatisfied, as we discover that possessions cannot fill the void of true happiness.

Even in our personal relationships, excess can be harmful. Overextending ourselves to please others, sacrificing our own needs and desires, or giving too much of our time and energy can lead to burnout, resentment, and emotional exhaustion.

harmony. By embracing moderation and avoiding the temptations of excess, we can lead a life of purpose, clarity, and true happiness.

The Tale of Gautam Buddha and the Broken Vase: A story which explains how expectation hurts

In a small village nestled in the foothills of the Himalayas, a woman named Sujata invited Gautam Buddha and his followers for a meal. As she prepared her humble offering, her prized possession—a delicate porcelain vase—held water for the guests. The vase was a family heirloom, and Sujata cherished it dearly.

While the meal was being served, a young monk accidentally knocked over the vase. It shattered into countless pieces, and a heavy silence fell over the gathering. Tears welled in Sujata's eyes as she stared at the fragments on the floor.

Seeing her distress, Gautam Buddha gently spoke. "Sujata, why are you upset?"

"The vase is broken, O Enlightened One," she replied. "It was precious to me, a reminder of my ancestors. I had hoped it would last forever."

Buddha smiled gently and asked, "Did you expect that something so fragile could truly last forever?"

Sujata was silent, unsure how to respond.

Buddha continued, "All things in this world are impermanent. When we attach ourselves to them and expect them to remain unchanged, we set ourselves up for suffering. The vase, beautiful as it was, was always destined to break one day. Its nature was to be temporary. Your pain arises not from the vase breaking, but from your expectation that it never would."

Sujata listened intently, and the weight of his words began to sink in. She realized her sorrow came from clinging to an illusion of permanence.

Buddha then addressed the gathering, "Just as the vase was destined to shatter, so too are our relationships, possessions, and even our bodies impermanent. When we accept this truth, we free ourselves from unnecessary suffering. Let us cherish what we have in the present moment, knowing that change is the law of life."

The villagers were deeply moved by his wisdom. Sujata gathered the broken pieces of the vase, her heart lighter now. She thanked Buddha for helping her see beyond her attachment.

As the group departed, Sujata placed the fragments in her garden. Over time, they became part of a mosaic that reminded her not of loss, but of life's fleeting beauty and the peace that comes with letting go of expectations.

Expectations can lead to pain when reality doesn't align with them. True peace lies in embracing impermanence and finding joy in the present moment.

When Sujata lamented the loss of her vase, Gautam Buddha imparted wisdom about impermanence and the suffering caused by expectations. Interestingly, this concept aligns closely with the Second Law of

Thermodynamics, which states that entropy, or disorder, in an isolated system will always increase over time.

The vase, in its pristine state, represented order—a carefully crafted object of beauty and utility. However, when the monk accidentally shattered it, the vase transitioned into a state of higher entropy. Its broken pieces are scattered across the floor, illustrating the natural progression from order to chaos.

Just as the vase was destined to break due to its fragility, the Second Law of Thermodynamics teaches us that all systems inherently move toward greater disorder unless external energy is applied to maintain or restore order.

Sujata's grief stemmed from her expectation that the vase would remain intact forever. This expectation was, in essence, a denial of entropy—a refusal to acknowledge the natural tendency toward disorder and impermanence.

Buddha's wisdom aligns with the scientific principle: just as one cannot halt the progression of entropy in physical systems, one cannot cling to the illusion of permanence in life. Recognizing and accepting the inevitability of change allows us to navigate life's disruptions with equanimity.

Buddha's teaching encourages us to find peace in the reality of impermanence, just as scientists accept entropy as a fundamental law of the universe. Rather than resist chaos or mourn the loss of order, we can reframe our perspective to appreciate the beauty of fleeting moments and adapt to the natural progression of change.

Sujata, by transforming the shattered vase into a mosaic for her garden, embraced this concept. She didn't fight the inevitable increase in disorder but instead used it as an opportunity to create something meaningful, symbolizing how even chaos can lead to new forms of order and understanding.

The Conclusion of the story reflects the Second Law of Thermodynamics: chaos (or entropy) will always increase over time. Buddha's lesson teaches us to accept this universal truth and let go of expectations for permanence. By aligning our understanding of life with the laws of nature, we can find harmony amidst the universe's inevitable changes.

The Concept of Relativity: A Perspective-Shifting Idea

The concept of relativity, primarily introduced by Albert Einstein, fundamentally changed how we understand the universe. At its core, relativity suggests that there is no universal, absolute perspective for time, space, or motion. Instead, these measurements depend on the observer's frame of reference. This concept can profoundly influence how we perceive not only the physical universe but also the subjective experiences of individuals.

Key Principles of Relativity

Special Relativity

Einstein's Special Theory of Relativity (1905) is based on two key ideas:

The Speed of Light is Constant: The speed of light (approximately 299,792 km/s) is the same for all observers, regardless of their motion relative to the light source.

Time and Space Are Relative: Time and space are not fixed; they vary depending on the observer's speed and perspective. For instance:

A moving clock ticks slower compared to a stationary one (time dilation).

Objects appear shorter in the direction of motion when moving close to the speed of light (length contraction).

General Relativity

Einstein extended these ideas in 1915 to include gravity:

Gravity Warps Space-Time: Massive objects like planets or stars bend the fabric of space-time, creating what we perceive as gravity.

Perspective Shifts Due to Gravity: Time runs slower near massive objects (gravitational time dilation). For instance, a clock closer to a planet's surface ticks more slowly than one farther away.

How Relativity Changes Perspectives

Relativity not only explains the universe's mechanics but also reshapes how we think about individual perspectives—both scientifically and philosophically:

There's No Absolute Reality: How Perspectives Shape and Are Shaped by Physics

The idea that "there's no absolute reality" arises directly from the principles of relativity in physics and finds profound parallels in human experience. It suggests that reality is not a single, fixed truth shared identically by all observers. Instead, reality is shaped by the observer's position, motion, and environment.

Physics provides the framework for understanding how different perspectives are not only possible but intrinsic to the structure of the universe. Here's how this principle operates in physics and translates to human perspectives:

Relativity in Physics: A Universe Without Absolutes

Space and Time Are Relative
Einstein's theories of relativity demonstrate that:
Time and space depend on the observer. Two observers in different frames of reference—one stationary, one moving—will measure time and distance differently. For example:
A person traveling at near-light speed will experience time more slowly compared to someone stationary (time dilation).
An object moving at high speeds will appear shorter along its direction of motion (length contraction).
This shows that even fundamental aspects of the universe, like time and space, have no universal standard—they're relative to each observer's perspective.

In quantum mechanics, the observer's role becomes even more critical. The famous double-slit experiment shows that whether light behaves like a particle or a wave depends on how it's observed. This implies that observation itself influences the manifestation of physical phenomena.

These principles reveal that the universe allows for multiple "realities," each valid in its own frame of reference.

Shaping Perspectives: Why Everyone Sees Reality Differently

Just as physics accommodates different realities based on an observer's frame of reference, human perspectives are shaped by personal factors, including:

Cultural Background: Someone raised in one culture may interpret a situation entirely differently from someone in another.

Emotional State: A person in a calm, content state may see an event as trivial, while someone in distress may view it as catastrophic.

Knowledge and Experience: Understanding colors and how we interpret events; for instance, a scientist may see beauty in a complex equation, while someone unfamiliar with mathematics may see it as incomprehensible.

Just as a moving observer in physics perceives time and space differently, a person actively engaged in an experience interprets it differently from someone passively observing. For instance, a player in a sports game and a spectator in the stands have very different realities of the same event.

Similar to gravitational effects in relativity, external influences—such as societal norms or immediate surroundings—warp individual perspectives. Someone living in an urban setting might see nature as a luxury, while someone in a rural area might see it as a mundane part of life.

Physics Permits Diverse Perspectives

In general relativity, all frames of reference are equally valid. Whether you're stationary on Earth or moving in a spaceship, your measurements and experiences are real and correct from your point of view. This parallels how human perspectives, shaped by unique contexts, are equally valid in their own right.

Two observers can disagree about the order of events if they're moving relative to each other. For instance, in relativistic speeds, one observer might see Event A happen before Event B, while another sees the reverse. Yet, both perspectives are valid within the laws of physics.

In physics, no "master clock" governs time universally. Similarly, no "master truth" governs human perspectives. The laws of the universe inherently allow for diverse and equally valid views of reality, both scientifically and philosophically.

Implications for Human Understanding

Recognizing that there's no absolute reality helps us appreciate that others' perspectives, even when they differ from ours, are just as valid. Physics teaches us that disagreement doesn't negate truth; it simply reflects different frames of reference.

Understanding that perspectives are shaped by context and position fosters empathy. Just as scientists work to reconcile different observational data to understand the universe, humans can work together to find common ground, even when starting from vastly different viewpoints.

In physics, perspectives shift with motion or gravitational fields. Similarly, human perspectives evolve with experience and knowledge. By embracing this dynamic nature of reality, we can adapt more effectively to change and uncertainty.

The universe, through its laws of physics, invites us to view reality not as a singular, immutable truth but as a tapestry woven from countless perspectives. Each observer, whether in science or in life, contributes a unique thread to this tapestry.

By understanding that "there is no absolute reality," we can better navigate the complexities of the universe and human relationships, appreciating the richness of diversity in both science and experience.

Time is Subjective

Relativity shows that time flows differently depending on speed and gravity. Philosophically, this underscores how each person's perception of time varies. For instance, time may feel slower when you're bored and faster when you're happy—an everyday manifestation of relativity.

Empathy Through Relativity

Understanding that everyone has their own "frame of reference" fosters empathy. Just as two observers can measure time differently depending on their motion, individuals may interpret situations differently based on their background and circumstances.

Expanding Horizons

Relativity encourages questioning assumptions about reality. It invites us to look beyond rigid, fixed ideas and consider that the universe—and human experience—is far more nuanced and interconnected than it first appears.

Relativity in Everyday Life

Travel and Technology:
GPS satellites account for both special relativity (due to their high speed) and general relativity (due to their position in weaker gravitational fields). Without these corrections, navigation errors would accumulate rapidly.

Interpersonal Relationships

In relationships, misunderstandings often arise because people view the same situation differently. Relativity reminds us that each person's "reality" is shaped by their frame of reference.

Art and Interpretation

Just as motion and time are relative, so is art. A single piece of art can evoke joy in one person and sorrow in another, depending on their emotional and cultural lens.

Relativity isn't just a scientific theory—it's a profound reminder that perspective matters. Whether in physics or life, reality depends on where you stand and how you move. Recognizing this can make us more understanding, adaptable, and curious about the diverse experiences of others.

Relativity challenges us to see the world not as fixed and absolute, but as a dynamic tapestry of interconnected perspectives.

Power of Consistency

We have already seen the concept of Coming back tomorrow in chapter 2. Success, in any field—be it fitness, career, learning, or relationships—requires consistency. The phrase, "The secret of success is to come back tomorrow," captures the essence of this principle. It emphasizes that progress is not about grand, one-time efforts but about showing up regularly and committing to the process over time.

Consistency means repeatedly engaging in actions aligned with your goals, even when motivation wavers or results seem distant. It's about steady effort, persistence, and the ability to follow through on commitments daily, regardless of circumstances.

How "Coming Back Tomorrow" Reflects Consistency

Small Steps Build Momentum

One extraordinary effort might give you a brief sense of accomplishment, but it's the accumulation of small, consistent actions that leads to sustainable progress. Showing up day after day allows you to build habits, refine skills, and create lasting change.

For example:

In fitness, doing a moderate workout daily builds stamina better than a single intense session followed by burnout.

In learning, studying for 30 minutes every day is more effective than cramming for 10 hours before an exam.

Overcoming Obstacles and Plateaus

Consistency teaches resilience. When you commit to "coming back tomorrow," you learn to push through challenges, moments of doubt, and plateaus. Over time, these struggles become stepping stones rather than barriers.

Compounding Effects of Effort

Like compound interest in finance, which we have already seen in the chapter-4 Money, the benefits of consistent effort multiply over time. Each small action builds on the previous one, leading to exponential growth in skills, strength, or success.

The Importance of Consistency

Consistency bridges the gap between effort and results. While an intense effort might feel satisfying in the short term, it is the daily, incremental progress that transforms goals into achievements.

Motivation is fleeting and unpredictable; some days, you won't feel like putting in the work. Consistency, however, relies on discipline—the commitment to show up, no matter how you feel. This discipline becomes a habit, making success inevitable.

Being consistent builds self-confidence because you prove to yourself that you can commit to and follow through on goals. It also builds trust with others, as people see you as dependable and reliable.

Whether in personal growth, career, or relationships, consistency creates a strong foundation. It's not the grand gestures but the daily acts—of kindness, effort, or diligence—that lead to enduring success.

Practical Applications of "Come Back Tomorrow"

In Fitness:
Instead of overtraining one day and skipping the next, commit to manageable daily workouts. Even on rest days, do light stretches or a short walk to maintain the habit.

In Learning:
Study or practice a skill daily, even if only for a few minutes. Consistency ensures retention and gradual improvement.

In Career:
Show up for your work, even on challenging days. Regular effort and small improvements accumulate to build expertise and credibility.

In Relationships:
Invest in relationships daily through small acts of kindness, communication, and understanding. Consistency strengthens bonds over time.

The beauty of "coming back tomorrow" is its simplicity. It doesn't demand perfection or extraordinary effort; it simply asks for persistence. You don't have to achieve everything today—you just need to commit to trying again tomorrow.

When you embrace this mindset,

Failures become temporary, as there's always another chance.

Progress feels achievable, as it's broken down into manageable steps.

The journey itself becomes rewarding, as you focus on showing up rather than fixating on the outcome.

Consistency is the foundation of success. By adopting the mindset that "the secret of success is to come back tomorrow," you commit to steady, incremental growth. This approach transforms overwhelming goals into achievable realities, builds resilience, and creates lasting habits.

Success is not a destination reached in one giant leap but a path paved by the small, repeated steps you take every single day. So, no matter how today goes, remember: "Come back tomorrow."

The Persistent Farmer: The Secret of Success

In a small village surrounded by rolling hills, there lived a farmer named Keshav. Every year, he planted crops in his modest field, hoping for a good harvest. One year, a severe drought struck the region. Despite his best efforts, Keshav's crops began to wither, and the villagers advised him to abandon the field, saying it was futile to try any longer.

But Keshav refused to give up. Each morning, he rose before dawn, carried buckets of water from a distant well, and carefully tended to his parched crops. Day after day, he worked tirelessly, even as others mocked his determination.

One morning, after weeks of effort, dark clouds gathered in the sky. Rain poured down, soaking the land. Keshav's crops, though weak, began to revive. When the harvest season arrived, Keshav reaped a modest but sufficient yield, enough to sustain his family.

The villagers were amazed. "How did you manage to succeed when the rest of us failed?" they asked.

Keshav smiled and said, "The secret of success is simple: I come back tomorrow. No matter how hard today was, I showed up again the next day. Little by little, my effort added up, and nature met me halfway."

Success often hinges on persistence. Challenges and setbacks are inevitable, but the key to overcoming them is the willingness to try again. Each "tomorrow" offers a new opportunity to make progress. Like the farmer, those who show up consistently, even when circumstances seem dire, set themselves apart.

So, the secret of success is simple: "Come back tomorrow." Keep showing up, keep trying, and over time, perseverance will bear fruit.

Finding Balance: The Key to a Fulfilling Life

Life is a delicate dance between competing priorities, desires, and responsibilities. Whether it's balancing work and personal life, ambition, and contentment, or health and indulgence, the ability to find equilibrium is essential for leading a fulfilling and meaningful existence. Striking the right balance enables us to thrive without feeling overwhelmed, stagnant, or dissatisfied.

Balance is not about giving equal time and energy to every aspect of life. Instead, it's about allocating your resources—time, effort, attention—in a way that aligns with your values, needs, and goals. It's recognizing that life is dynamic, and priorities may shift over time, requiring constant adjustment.

Why Balance is Important

Prevents Burnout
Overcommitting to one area, such as work, can lead to physical and emotional exhaustion. Balance ensures that no single aspect of life drains all your energy, leaving you refreshed and motivated.

Enhances Well-Being
Balance contributes to mental, emotional, and physical health.

For example:
Taking time for relaxation and hobbies reduces stress.
Prioritizing relationships fosters emotional fulfillment.
Ensuring work-life harmony prevents feelings of neglect or regret.

Promotes Growth
When life is balanced, you create space for personal growth. This might mean learning new skills, nurturing relationships, or exploring passions that would otherwise be overshadowed by a singular focus.

Fosters Joy and Fulfillment
A balanced life allows you to enjoy the present while working toward the future. It keeps you grounded in what truly matters and helps you savor small joys.

Areas Where Balance is Crucial

Work and Personal Life
Imbalance: Overworking leads to neglected relationships, poor health, and emotional fatigue.
Solution: Set boundaries, prioritize quality time with loved ones, and practice self-care.

Ambition and Contentment
Imbalance: Constant striving without appreciating achievements can leave you feeling unfulfilled.
Solution: Celebrate milestones while setting realistic goals.

Health and Enjoyment
Imbalance: Overemphasis on discipline can make life feel rigid, while overindulgence can harm well-being.
Solution: Balance healthy habits with occasional treats or relaxation.

Independence and Relationships
Imbalance: Too much independence may lead to isolation, while over-

reliance on others can hinder personal growth.
Solution: Maintain personal autonomy while nurturing meaningful connections.

Stability and Change
Imbalance: Clinging to routine can stifle growth, while constant change can create instability.
Solution: Embrace a stable foundation while remaining open to new experiences.

Challenges to Finding Balance

Perfectionism

The belief that everything must be done perfectly can make balance seem unattainable. Strive for progress, not perfection.

External Pressures

Societal expectations, peer pressure, or workplace demands can push you toward imbalance. Learn to prioritize your values over external approval.

Unrealistic Expectations

Balance doesn't mean you'll always feel at peace. Accept that some days will be more challenging than others.

Benefits of a Balanced Life

Improved Relationships: When you allocate time and energy to loved ones, you build stronger, more meaningful connections.

Enhanced Productivity: A well-rested and fulfilled mind is more focused and efficient.

Greater Resilience: Balance reduces stress and equips you to handle life's challenges with grace.

Lasting Fulfillment: Living in alignment with your values fosters a sense of purpose and contentment.

Imagine walking a tightrope: leaning too far in one direction can lead to a fall. Similarly, life requires constant adjustments to stay steady. Balance doesn't mean avoiding extremes entirely but recognizing when to lean in and when to pull back.

For instance:
After an intense work week, prioritize rest or family time over extra hours in the office.

If you've indulged during a vacation, return to healthier routines afterward.

Finding balance is a journey, not a destination. It's about learning to harmonize the various aspects of life in a way that reflects your values and promotes well-being. By striving for balance, you cultivate resilience, embrace joy, and build a life that feels meaningful and fulfilling.

Remember, the key isn't doing everything perfectly—it's doing what matters consistently and with intention. In the dance of life, balance is what keeps us moving gracefully.

The Power of Moderation: A Path to a Balanced and Fulfilling Life

Moderation, the practice of avoiding extremes and finding the middle ground, is a principle deeply rooted in philosophy, religion, and science. It involves striking a balance between indulgence and restraint, allowing us to enjoy life's pleasures while maintaining health, stability, and long-term success.

In a world often defined by excess or deprivation, moderation stands as a guiding principle for achieving harmony in every aspect of life.

Moderation means making choices that are neither excessive nor insufficient. It's about temperance—engaging with life's experiences in a balanced and thoughtful way. This doesn't mean avoiding enjoyment or challenges but rather ensuring that neither dominates to the detriment of overall well-being.

The Philosophical and Scientific Basis of Moderation

Aristotle's "Golden Mean"

Aristotle described moderation as the "golden mean" between two extremes—excess and deficiency. For example:

Courage lies between recklessness and cowardice.
Generosity lies between wastefulness and stinginess.

Moderation, according to Aristotle, is the foundation of virtue and leads to a flourishing life.

Biological Balance

The human body thrives on balance:
Overeating leads to obesity; undereating leads to malnutrition.
Overworking leads to burnout; underworking leads to stagnation.
Moderation aligns with the body's natural rhythms, optimizing health and performance.

Modern Psychology
Studies show that people who practice moderation are happier and less stressed. Overindulgence can lead to guilt, while extreme restraint can cause frustration. Moderation fosters satisfaction and sustainable habits.

The Power of Moderation in Different Areas of Life

Physical Health
Moderation in diet, exercise, and sleep is key to physical well-being.
Diet: Overindulgence in unhealthy foods can lead to weight gain, while

extreme dieting can cause deficiencies. A balanced diet ensures both enjoyment and nutrition.

Exercise: Overtraining can lead to injuries, while lack of exercise causes poor health. A moderate, consistent routine builds strength and endurance sustainably.

Emotional Well-Being

Emotional moderation means neither suppressing feelings nor being overwhelmed by them.

It allows for the healthy expression of emotions while maintaining composure.

Practicing moderation in responses—neither overreacting nor being apathetic—fosters better relationships and personal growth.

Finances

Moderation in spending and saving is essential for financial stability.

Overspending leads to debt, while extreme frugality can cause unnecessary stress and missed opportunities for enjoyment.

Balanced financial planning ensures security and allows for occasional indulgences.

Work-Life Balance

Moderation in work prevents burnout and ensures time for personal life.

Working too much can strain health and relationships.

Working too little can hinder progress and fulfillment.

Finding a balance allows for professional success and personal happiness.

Technology and Social Media

Moderation in technology use prevents digital addiction and fosters real-world connections.

Excessive screen time harms mental health and relationships.

Avoiding technology entirely can isolate you from modern opportunities.

Moderate usage ensures productivity and meaningful engagement.

Personal Growth

Moderation in ambition helps balance striving for success with appreciating the present.

Overemphasis on achievement can cause stress and dissatisfaction.

Too little ambition can lead to stagnation.
A moderate approach keeps you motivated while enjoying life's journey.

The Benefits of Moderation

Sustainability
Moderation allows habits and practices to be maintained over the long term.
Extreme efforts, while impactful in the short term, are often unsustainable.

Greater Satisfaction
Moderation fosters contentment. By avoiding the extremes of overindulgence or deprivation, you can enjoy life's pleasures without guilt or regret.

Improved Decision-Making
A moderate mindset encourages thoughtful, balanced decisions rather than impulsive or overly cautious choices.

Enhanced Relationships
Moderation in expectations, communication, and behaviors strengthens relationships by promoting fairness and understanding.

Inner Peace
Moderation reduces the highs and lows of extreme living, creating a steadier, more peaceful state of mind.

How to Cultivate Moderation

Practice Mindfulness

Be aware of your habits and decisions. Ask yourself: Am I leaning too far into indulgence or restriction?

Set Realistic Boundaries
Define limits for activities like eating, working, or spending, ensuring they align with your values and goals.

Learn from Experience
Reflect on past experiences of excess or deprivation to identify what works best for you.

Embrace Flexibility
Moderation isn't rigid. Allow room for occasional indulgences or extra effort when needed, as long as balance is restored.

Seek Balance, Not Perfection
Moderation isn't about being perfect; it's about finding what feels right in the moment and adapting as life changes.

The Paradox of Moderation

While moderation is about balance, it doesn't mean avoiding intensity when it's needed. There are times when intense focus, effort, or indulgence may be appropriate. The key is to recognize when to push hard and when to pull back.

For example:
In times of crisis, you may need to work intensely, but moderation ensures you don't exhaust yourself in the long term.

Celebrations may call for indulgence, but moderation ensures that these moments remain special rather than habitual.

Moderation is not about limiting joy or ambition but enhancing it by creating balance. It allows us to experience the richness of life without being overwhelmed by its extremes. Whether in health, relationships, work, or personal growth, moderation provides a framework for sustainable success and happiness.

As the ancient saying goes, "**Everything in moderation, including moderation itself.**" Life is a dynamic journey, and moderation is the compass that guides us through its complexities toward a fulfilling and harmonious existence.

We are now heading towards the last chapter of this book, which is going to surprise you as we are now going to talk about Addition rather than Elimination.

CHAPTER EIGHT

ADDITION

In the previous chapters, we explored the immense value of elimination in achieving peace, clarity, and focus. By eliminating bad habits, toxic relationships, and unnecessary distractions, we create space in our lives for growth and self-improvement. However, elimination is only a first step towards growth. Rather a back step to prepare for a long jump. Once we remove the negative elements, a vacuum is created, and that space must be filled. This is where the concept of Addition comes into play.

Addition isn't just about randomly filling that space with new things. It's about carefully, thoughtfully, and deliberately choosing what to bring into our lives, whether it be habits, relationships, or experiences. If the space created by elimination isn't filled wisely, the same destructive patterns can easily creep back in, perpetuating a vicious cycle.

This chapter emphasizes the importance of mindful Addition and how to integrate new, positive habits and people into your life. The goal is to ensure that the progress you've made through elimination isn't undone but rather enhanced by what you choose to add.

The Vacant Space After Elimination

After successfully eliminating negative habits or people from our lives, we often experience a sense of freedom, lightness, and clarity. However, this newfound space can feel unsettling or incomplete. Our minds and environments, by their very nature, seek to fill gaps. If this void isn't filled with something positive, it can easily be occupied by yet another bad habit, toxic relationship, or unnecessary distraction.

For instance, let's say you've eliminated the habit of binge-watching TV shows late at night. Suddenly, you find yourself with several extra hours in the evening. If you don't proactively decide how to use this time, you might end up scrolling through social media for hours or finding some other equally unproductive activity. The key is to consciously decide what to add to that time so that it serves you and aligns with your goals.

But how do you go about this process of mindful addition?

Step 1: Identify the Gaps

The first step in transforming your life through the process of elimination is to identify the gaps created by removing negative habits, relationships, or behaviors. These gaps are opportunities for growth, renewal, and positive change. Whether you've given up smoking, left a toxic relationship, or eliminated distractions like excessive social media use, it's important to recognize the space this removal creates in your life.

For example, if you've quit smoking, you might suddenly find that you have extra time during the day that was once filled with smoke breaks. You'll notice physical benefits like fewer cravings and improved health, as well as financial savings. But the key is not just noticing what's missing; it's realizing the potential this newfound space holds. What will you do with the extra time and energy? The gap isn't a void to be feared—it's a canvas for you to fill with something that truly enriches your life.

Similarly, eliminating a toxic relationship can leave emotional gaps. Perhaps you were used to constant drama, stress, or conflict that consumed much of your mental energy. When the relationship ends, it's common to feel a sense of loss or emptiness, but within that emptiness lies a powerful opportunity. The emotional space that was once filled with negativity can now be used to cultivate healthier connections, work on personal growth, or focus on things that bring you joy.

Recognizing these gaps is essential because it prevents you from unconsciously slipping back into old habits or toxic patterns. Think of it like decluttering your home—when you clear out a room, you create physical space, but if you're not intentional about what you allow back in, that space will quickly fill with new clutter. The same principle applies to your life. If you don't consciously decide how to use the time, energy, and emotional space you've gained, you might fall into old routines or pick up new, equally unproductive habits.

By identifying and appreciating the gaps, you can mindfully choose what to add back into your life. Instead of allowing the void to pull you back into negative patterns, you can fill it with positive actions, healthy relationships, and habits that align with your goals and values. This awareness not only helps you maintain the progress you've made but also empowers you to build a life that's more intentional, fulfilling, and free from the clutter of unnecessary distractions.

Step 2: Add with Intention

When it comes to addition, the keyword is intention. It's not about rushing to fill the void with just anything; it's about carefully choosing what will truly enhance your life. The things you add should align with your values, goals, and desires.

For example, if you've stopped wasting time on social media, you might want to add a productive habit like reading. But don't rush into it. Consider what kinds of books would be most beneficial or enjoyable for you. If you're not sure where to start, you might begin by exploring different genres or asking for recommendations from trusted friends. The important thing is to avoid the temptation of adding something hastily, which could easily lead to another unproductive habit.

Incorporating a mentor or role model can help immensely during this process. A good mentor can provide guidance, share their experiences, and offer suggestions for what habits or practices might be beneficial for you. For instance, if you're trying to develop a new exercise routine, following the regimen of a fitness expert or personal trainer could save you time and provide direction.

Step 3: Replace Bad Habits with Good Ones

One of the most effective ways to solidify positive change is to directly replace bad habits with good ones. When you eliminate something negative, such as excessive TV watching or unhealthy eating, you should aim to introduce a healthier alternative.

Let's revisit the example of eliminating the habit of binge-watching TV shows. If you want to replace this habit with reading, make sure to plan how you will go about it. Start small—perhaps by dedicating just 30 minutes each evening to reading. Over time, this habit will grow stronger, and you'll likely find yourself reading for longer periods without even thinking about it.

The process of replacing habits doesn't have to be complicated, but it does require consistency. As James Clear discusses in his book Atomic Habits, there are four key steps to building a new habit:

Make it obvious – Make the new habit visible. If you want to read more, keep books around your living space where they are easily accessible.

Make it attractive – Choose books that genuinely interest you, so that reading feels enjoyable, not like a chore.

Make it easy – Start with something manageable. If reading for an hour feels too overwhelming, start with 10 minutes a day.

Make it satisfying – Reward yourself for sticking to the habit. Celebrate your progress, whether that's finishing a book or simply completing your reading goal for the week.

By following these steps, you ensure that the new habit sticks and doesn't get replaced by another bad one.

Step 4: Be Mindful of Your Surroundings

When trying to introduce positive changes into your life, it's important to be mindful of your surroundings. If you're in the same environment where your old habits were formed, it can be difficult to make lasting changes. Your surroundings influence your behavior more than you might realize.

For example, if you used to spend hours watching TV in your living room, it might be helpful to create a dedicated reading nook in a different part of your home. Similarly, if you used to associate your office space with stress or distraction, make small changes to it—such as adding plants or rearranging the furniture—to create a more positive, productive atmosphere.

As the saying goes, "One space, one use." When your brain associates a specific space with a particular activity, it's easier to stay focused and avoid distractions. Having a designated workspace, a place for relaxation, and an area for exercise or hobbies can help you maintain balance and reinforce positive habits.

Step 5: Fail Fast and Correct

One of the most significant obstacles to growth is the fear of failure. This fear often holds people back, preventing them from taking action or trying something new. We tend to associate failure with a lack of competence or worth, but in reality, failure is one of the most powerful tools for learning and progress. The key to overcoming this fear is to fail fast and correct—an approach that embraces mistakes as part of the journey and allows for quick adaptation.

Consider the story of Thomas Edison, who conducted thousands of experiments before finally discovering the right material to make the lightbulb filament. He didn't view his failed attempts as setbacks but as stepping stones. Each failure taught him something valuable, ruling out one more method that didn't work and bringing him closer to the one that did. This mindset of persistence and learning from failure is what ultimately led to his success.

In the same way, when you're trying to add new habits, activities, or relationships into your life, it's essential to embrace trial and error. Suppose you're trying to pick up a new hobby, like painting, or learning a new language. You might not be great at it right away, and that's okay. The process of attempting, failing, and adjusting will eventually guide you toward improvement. The goal isn't to avoid mistakes but to learn from them as quickly as possible.

When you "fail fast," you don't dwell on your missteps; you make a decision, test it, and if it doesn't work, you course-correct. For example, say you've started a new fitness routine but quickly realize it's not sustainable or enjoyable. Instead of quitting altogether, you can swiftly adapt—perhaps by choosing a different form of exercise that suits your lifestyle better. This approach prevents wasted time and keeps you on a path of continuous improvement.

Similarly, relationships can also follow this pattern. You might meet new people, thinking they will bring positivity into your life, only to find that the relationship is draining or misaligned with your values. Recognizing this early on allows you to make adjustments—either by communicating boundaries, stepping back, or seeking new connections. The quicker you recognize what's not working, the quicker you can pivot toward something that does.

The essence of "failing fast and correcting" lies in experimentation. By not fearing failure, you gain the freedom to try new things without the burden of perfection. It becomes easier to tweak and refine your actions and decisions until you find the right fit. The faster you accept failure as part of the process, the faster you can move toward success. This mindset allows you to navigate challenges with resilience and an open mind, ultimately leading to personal growth and lasting achievements.

Step 6: Practice Daily and Focus on One Thing

In the journey of self-improvement and habit formation, one of the most critical steps is consistency. The act of committing to something daily, no matter how small, creates momentum that leads to lasting change. Think of it like planting a seed — the seed needs daily sunlight, water, and care to grow into a strong, healthy tree. Similarly, when you commit to practicing a habit every day, you're nurturing that habit to grow stronger over time.

The book 'The One Thing' by Gary Keller and Jay Papasan stresses the importance of focusing on a single task or goal at a time. In a world filled with distractions, it's tempting to multitask or try to achieve many things at once. However, The One Thing suggests that true progress is made by channeling your energy into just one important task, rather than scattering your attention across multiple areas. This focused effort allows you to make steady, meaningful progress, no matter how small the steps may seem.

When you practice daily, the results are like dominos stacked in a row — each small action builds on the previous one, leading to a powerful chain reaction. For example, if you want to learn a new language, spending just 10 minutes every day practicing vocabulary or grammar can accumulate significant mastery over months. Similarly, if you aim to get fit, even a short workout every day builds muscle memory, strength, and endurance.

Moreover, daily practice is about more than just repeating an action; it's about creating a habit loop. Initially, it might feel difficult to integrate a new activity into your day, but with persistence, it becomes automatic. This loop, once established, requires less effort and discipline to maintain because the habit has become part of your daily routine. Whether it's exercising, meditating, reading, or learning a new skill, each day you practice reinforces the habit and makes it a natural part of your life.

The power of focusing on one thing daily lies in its simplicity. Instead of being overwhelmed by the need to change everything at once, you can focus on just one habit or goal, giving it the attention and effort it needs to flourish. This focused, deliberate practice sets the foundation for long-term success. By concentrating on one thing at a time and practicing it every day, you can achieve mastery, creating profound and lasting transformation in your life.

Let's understand these steps through the story of Emily, A Journey from Bad Habits to Growth and Success

Emily was a talented graphic designer, but despite her creativity and potential, she often felt stuck in a cycle of bad habits. She spent too much time scrolling through social media, procrastinating on projects, and staying up late watching Netflix. Though she had dreams of starting her own design business, her daily routine was filled with distractions that kept her from making real progress.

One day, Emily hit a breaking point. She realized that her current habits weren't helping her move forward, and if she wanted to achieve her goals, she needed to make a change. Following a structured approach, Emily set out on a journey to eliminate her bad habits and replace them with positive, growth-oriented behaviors. Here's how she did it, step by step.

Step 1: Identify the Gaps

Emily knew her habits were holding her back, but she needed to understand where the gaps in her life were. She started by analyzing her daily routine and identified that the biggest gap in her life was the time she wasted on social media and streaming platforms. This mindless behavior was robbing her of hours that she could have used to work on her goals. Once she identified this gap, she realized that her life was full of potential opportunities—time that she could spend developing her design skills and building her business.

Step 2: Add with Intention

With a clear understanding of the time she could reclaim, Emily knew she had to add with intention. She didn't want to fill her newly available time with just any activity; she wanted to focus on what would drive her toward her goals. Emily decided to dedicate her evenings to working on her design portfolio and learning new tools like animation and 3D modeling. She set specific goals for each week, making sure that everything she added to her routine aligned with her long-term vision of becoming a successful entrepreneur in the design industry.

Step 3: Replace Bad Habits with Good Ones

Emily knew that eliminating bad habits wasn't enough—she needed to replace them with good ones. So instead of spending hours on social media every night, she began to block off time for learning and working on her portfolio. She also replaced her habit of staying up late watching TV with an evening routine of reading design blogs and books. This allowed her to build momentum around positive habits, making it easier to stick to her new routine. Soon, Emily found that her cravings for social media and TV were fading, and her desire to work on her designs grew stronger.

Step 4: Be Mindful of Your Surroundings

Emily recognized that her surroundings played a major role in her habits. Her living room, with the TV always on, was a constant trigger for procrastination. To support her new habits, she created a dedicated workspace in her apartment where she could focus on her design projects. She rearranged her desk, placed inspiring artwork on the walls, and filled the space with books and materials that encouraged creativity. By being mindful of her surroundings, Emily made sure that her environment supported her growth rather than triggering old, unproductive habits.

Step 5: Fail Fast and Correct

In the beginning, Emily wasn't perfect. She had moments where she slipped back into old habits, such as binge-watching her favorite shows or scrolling endlessly through Instagram. However, instead of letting these moments derail her progress, she embraced the principle of failing fast and correcting. Each time she slipped, she would reflect on what caused her to falter and make adjustments to her plan. For example, she realized that she needed to be more strict about setting a "screen-free" time after 8 PM. These quick adjustments helped her stay on track and grow without getting stuck in guilt or frustration.

Step 6: Practice Daily and Focus on One Thing

To ensure her new habits stuck, Emily knew she had to commit to daily practice. She set a goal to spend at least two hours every evening working on her designs and portfolio, focusing on one project at a time. This daily discipline not only improved her skills but also built her confidence. As she focused on one task each day—whether it was learning a new animation technique or designing a client proposal—Emily noticed steady progress. The key to her success was consistency, and by sticking to this focused routine, she began to see tangible results.

The Results

Over time, Emily's dedication paid off. She successfully built an impressive portfolio, gained freelance clients, and even started an online store selling her own custom designs. Her daily commitment to her craft, combined with her ability to quickly correct course when she made mistakes, fueled her growth. Emily's design business flourished, and she eventually left her 9-to-5 job to pursue her passion full-time.

By following these six steps, Emily transformed her life from one filled with distractions and bad habits into one focused on growth and success. Her story is a powerful reminder that with intention, discipline, and a willingness to adapt, anyone can break free from bad habits and achieve their goals.

Invest in Your Skills: The Key to Personal and Financial Growth

Investing in your skills is one of the most valuable and sustainable ways to achieve personal and financial success. Unlike material assets, which may lose value over time, skills are an investment that can be appreciated and bring lifelong benefits. By continuously learning and improving, you open doors to new opportunities, increase your earning potential, and position yourself for long-term growth in a rapidly changing world.

Why Investing in Your Skills Matters:

Increased Earning Potential: The more skilled and knowledgeable you are, the more valuable you become in the marketplace. Employers are willing to pay more for individuals who have specialized skills, certifications, or advanced expertise in their field. Whether it's mastering a technical skill, learning a new language, or gaining leadership abilities, investing in your education can directly translate into higher income.

Job Security and Flexibility: In an era of automation, technological advancements, and shifting job markets, having a diverse and adaptable skill set is crucial for staying relevant. Continuous learning ensures you're not left behind as industries evolve. By expanding your skill set, you can move more easily between roles, industries, or even career paths. This flexibility gives you greater control over your professional life and can help you weather economic downturns or changes in your current job.

Opportunities for Advancement: Acquiring new skills not only makes you more competent but also positions you for promotions and leadership roles. Whether it's soft skills like communication and teamwork or hard skills like coding and data analysis, employers often seek individuals who demonstrate a willingness to grow. Investing in these areas can make you a top candidate for higher-level positions and responsibilities.

Entrepreneurial Growth: If you're an entrepreneur or aspire to start your own business, investing in skills like marketing, financial management, and digital tools can help you succeed. Entrepreneurship requires a broad set of skills, and those who continuously invest in learning and self-improvement are more likely to navigate challenges and capitalize on opportunities.

Ways to Invest in Your Skills:

Formal Education:

Enroll in Higher Education: Earning a degree or certification in a relevant field can provide specialized knowledge and credentials that enhance your career prospects.

Take Online Courses: Platforms like Coursera, Udemy, and LinkedIn Learning offer affordable courses on everything from computer programming to leadership skills. These are convenient ways to upgrade your abilities without committing to a full-time program.

Workshops and Seminars:

Attend Industry Conferences: Participate in workshops or seminars to gain insights from experts, learn about the latest trends, and expand your professional network.

Certifications and Licenses: Certain professions offer certifications that demonstrate your competence in specific areas, such as project management, IT, or finance. Obtaining these credentials can set you apart from others in your field.

On-the-Job Learning:

Seek Mentorship: Working closely with experienced professionals allows you to learn industry-specific knowledge and gain invaluable advice that can't be taught in a classroom.

Job Rotations and Stretch Assignments: Ask for opportunities within your current role to take on new challenges or switch to different departments. This broadens your experience and helps develop diverse competencies.

Personal Development:

Develop Soft Skills: Skills like emotional intelligence, time management, and adaptability are just as important as technical abilities. Soft skills help you navigate complex social and workplace environments.

Read and Stay Informed: Reading industry publications, books, and research articles keeps you informed of new developments and equips you with a broader understanding of your field.

The Long-Term Benefits

Compounding Returns: Similar to how financial investments grow over time, the more you invest in your skills, the more returns you see. A single new skill can open doors to new opportunities, which in turn lead to further learning and growth. Over the course of a career, this creates a snowball effect of increasing value.

Fulfillment and Confidence: Mastering new skills and achieving personal milestones provides a sense of satisfaction. The confidence gained from learning something new or overcoming challenges enhances your overall well-being and motivates you to take on further challenges.

Financial Independence: Over time, investing in your skills can lead to higher salaries, better job opportunities, and even the potential to start your own business. This financial growth contributes to greater independence and security, enabling you to work on your terms and invest in other aspects of your life.

Living in the moment

In the book 12 Rules for Life, the 12th and final rule is "Pet a Cat When You Encounter One on the Street." This rule may seem whimsical at first, but it carries a profound and practical message about coping with the inevitable hardships of life. Peterson uses this metaphor to highlight the importance of finding small moments of beauty and solace amidst suffering and chaos. Here's why this rule is so vital:

Peterson emphasizes that suffering is an inherent part of existence. Life is unpredictable, and everyone will face pain, loss, or challenges at some point. Instead of denying or avoiding suffering, this rule encourages embracing life as it is while seeking small sources of relief and meaning.

The metaphor of petting a cat symbolizes pausing to appreciate the simple, fleeting joys in life—whether it's a kind gesture, a beautiful sunset, or the warmth of a loved one.

These small moments remind us that beauty and goodness still exist, even in the darkest times.

They serve as a buffer against despair, helping us stay grounded and hopeful.

This rule implicitly encourages mindfulness—the practice of being fully present in the moment.

By paying attention to the "cat on the street," you cultivate awareness and gratitude for the here and now.

Mindfulness reduces stress and anxiety, enabling you to better handle challenges without being overwhelmed.

Life's chaos can feel overwhelming when we focus on what we cannot control. The "cat" represents an opportunity to shift focus away from the uncontrollable to the immediate and tangible.

This shift helps build resilience by allowing you to accept life's unpredictability while finding meaning and joy in the small things.

When life feels heavy, small moments of joy can provide a glimpse of hope.

They remind you that life is not solely defined by hardship; it also includes moments of grace and wonder.

This broader perspective helps maintain emotional balance and prevents you from being consumed by negativity.

The rule also implies the importance of kindness, even to a stray cat. Small acts of compassion—for others or yourself—can bring profound relief and connection.

When you extend care to others, you contribute to their moment of solace as well, creating a ripple effect of positivity.

Practical Applications of the 12th Rule

Look for Small Joys Daily: Whether it's enjoying your morning coffee, listening to music, or spending time with a loved one, intentionally seek moments that bring happiness.

Pause and Appreciate the Present: Practice mindfulness by focusing on what is immediately around you, especially when life feels overwhelming.

Control Your Focus: Shift your attention away from what you can't change and toward what you can appreciate or improve.

Find Meaning in Challenges: Even amidst suffering, look for lessons, growth, or moments of relief.

Be Kind to Yourself and Others: Small acts of kindness, whether directed inward or outward, can help ease.

The 12th rule encapsulates the central theme of 12 Rules for Life: finding order, meaning, and resilience in a chaotic world. It offers a powerful reminder that while we cannot eliminate suffering, we can soften its impact by focusing on the beauty and goodness that persist in even the most trying times.

By embracing this mindset, we not only endure life's challenges but also cultivate a deeper appreciation for its richness and complexity. The "cat" serves as a metaphor for the moments that make life worth living, no matter how fleeting or small.

Dopamine: The Reward Hormone

Dopamine is a neurotransmitter (a chemical messenger in the brain) often referred to as the "reward hormone." It plays a crucial role in regulating mood, motivation, pleasure, and reward-seeking behaviors. Central to the brain's reward system, dopamine influences how we perceive pleasure and encourages us to repeat behaviors that lead to positive outcomes.

Key Functions of Dopamine

Reward and Pleasure: Dopamine is released when you experience something enjoyable or satisfying, like eating delicious food, achieving a goal, or receiving praise. This release reinforces the behavior, making you more likely to repeat it.

Motivation: Dopamine drives you to seek out rewards and accomplish tasks. It's often linked to the anticipation of a reward rather than the reward itself, which is why it fuels goal-directed behavior.

Focus and Attention: Dopamine helps regulate attention and focus. Adequate levels of dopamine are crucial for tasks that require concentration.

Learning and Memory: Dopamine strengthens learning by associating specific actions with positive outcomes. This process helps the brain remember what actions led to rewards in the past.

How Dopamine Works

Triggered by Stimuli: Certain activities, such as eating, exercising, or achieving goals, trigger dopamine release. This creates feelings of pleasure and satisfaction.

The Reward Circuit: Dopamine is part of the brain's reward system, which involves structures like the ventral tegmental area (VTA), nucleus accumbens, and prefrontal cortex. These areas communicate to produce the sensation of reward and motivate action.

Regulating Dopamine for Fulfillment

Throughout this book, we've emphasized the power of elimination—removing the unnecessary to create space for growth. One critical aspect of this process has been addressing dopamine addiction. In a world where instant gratification is at our fingertips, overindulgence in dopamine-driven habits—like excessive social media, junk food, or other quick fixes—can leave us drained and unfulfilled. Elimination helps break this cycle, allowing us to reset and reclaim control over our focus and energy.

However, the journey doesn't end there. Just as we eliminate excess, we must also be intentional about reintroducing dopamine into our lives in a balanced and meaningful way. Planning and incorporating small, consistent doses of dopamine through purposeful activities—like setting and achieving small goals, nurturing relationships, or exploring creative outlets—can lead to a more positive and fulfilling life.

The key lies in moderation and mindfulness. By adding these moments of joy and reward in smaller, deliberate quantities, we create a sustainable rhythm that energizes us without overwhelming our systems. This harmony between elimination and intentional addition transforms the way we experience life, shifting our focus from fleeting highs to enduring fulfillment.

Balancing Money and Dopamine

Saving money instead of spending it on things you love can often feel like a challenge. The allure of instant gratification—buying that new gadget, indulging in luxury items, or dining out frequently—offers a quick dopamine hit, making restraint difficult. However, as we've discussed throughout this book, eliminating impulsive behaviors and creating intentional habits pave the way for long-term growth and fulfillment.

One effective way to balance this is by planning your finances in a way that aligns with both responsibility and self-care. By consciously setting aside a portion of your income for savings and allocating a separate portion for self-care or small indulgences, you regulate the dopamine cycle in a healthy way.

This approach allows you to experience the joy and reward of treating yourself, without compromising on your financial goals. For example, splurging occasionally on a meaningful experience—like a relaxing spa day, a creative workshop, or a special meal—feels more fulfilling when it's planned and guilt-free. At the same time, watching your savings grow reinforces a sense of achievement and long-term security, providing a deeper, more sustained sense of satisfaction.

I suggest keeping 5% of your income for leisure activities that give you instant satisfaction and the energy to perform better the next day or week. Instead of creating a monthly budget, allot this money on a weekly basis so that you have consistent motivation throughout the month to navigate the "boringness" of the elimination phase.

Have you ever saved diligently for an emergency fund, only to feel depleted and crave something like a new bike or car? You might deserve that luxury, but not at the expense of your emergency fund. Without proper planning, you may end up using a portion of your emergency savings to buy a luxury item, only to realize that the dopamine high is temporary. Soon enough, you'll feel another craving for something bigger or better.

Dopamine makes you feel good at the moment, but it's crucial to remember that this feeling is fleeting. That's why feeding your dopamine in regular, planned intervals is important. Otherwise, unchecked cravings can destroy all the progress you've made so far. By maintaining balance and intentionality, you can satisfy your desire for reward while staying on track with your financial and personal growth goals.

Conclusion

As we come to the end of Eliminate: Chaos to Embrace Life, it is clear that the power of elimination goes far beyond simple decluttering—it is the foundation of personal growth and transformation. In this book, we've explored the various dimensions of life where elimination can serve as the first and most important step toward achieving clarity, focus, and fulfillment.

We began by addressing the chaos of information overload in our daily lives, where constant distractions and an overwhelming influx of data make it difficult to focus on what truly matters. By learning to set boundaries and be selective with what we allow into our minds, we gain control over our attention, reducing stress and enhancing our ability to engage meaningfully with the world around us.

In the realm of food and fitness, we explored how eliminating unhealthy habits and toxic patterns is crucial for reclaiming our physical health. We learned that by cutting out processed foods and reducing our reliance on instant gratification, we not only improve our bodies but also gain the mental strength to stay committed to long-term goals. Health and fitness, much like personal growth, require eliminating what no longer serves us in order to create space for practices that nourish and strengthen us.

Moving on to relationships, we examined the importance of eliminating toxic connections. We discussed how our personal growth is often held back by unhealthy relationships—whether they are draining friendships, controlling partnerships, or negative family dynamics. By identifying and removing these harmful influences, we allow room for healthier, more supportive relationships that align with our values and contribute positively to our journey.

In the dimension of money and financial freedom, we highlighted the significance of eliminating debt, impulsive spending, and poor financial habits. True financial success doesn't come from earning more or accumulating wealth but from learning to live within our means and making intentional, informed decisions. The power of elimination in our financial lives leads to long-term stability, independence, and peace of mind.

When it comes to work and productivity, we recognize that our success isn't determined by how busy we are but by how focused we are. By eliminating trivial tasks, pointless meetings, and unnecessary distractions, we create room for meaningful work. This focus on high-value tasks leads to greater productivity, creativity, and a deeper sense of accomplishment in our careers.

In the chapter on time affluence, we explored the concept of time as our most valuable resource. We understood that by eliminating time-wasting activities and focusing on what truly matters, we gain the freedom to live life more fully. Time affluence—having control over how we spend our time—is the key to a balanced and joyful life.

We also delved into the dangers of excess, examining how too much of anything—whether it's work, wealth, generosity, or even good habits—can lead to negative consequences. Moderation, paired with the wisdom of elimination, allows us to avoid the pitfalls of excess and maintain balance in every aspect of our lives.

Finally, we arrived at the concept of addition—the deliberate, mindful process of filling the space created by elimination. The journey doesn't end with cutting things out; true growth happens when we carefully and intentionally choose what to add back into our lives. Whether it's forming new habits, building stronger relationships, or pursuing passions that align with our purpose, mindful addition ensures that we continue to grow and thrive.

The overarching message of Eliminate: Chaos to Embrace Life is simple: to grow, we must first make space for growth. This book has shown that the process of elimination is not about deprivation but about clearing away the noise, distractions, and toxic influences that prevent us from living fully. It's about creating the mental, physical, and emotional space needed to focus on what truly matters and to build a life of purpose, meaning, and joy.

As you move forward in your own journey, remember that the first step toward achieving your goals, finding fulfillment, and living a balanced life begins with elimination. By consciously removing what no longer serves you, you empower yourself to embrace a life that is simpler, more intentional, and deeply rewarding.

Now, it's time to apply these principles to your own life and take the first step toward a future filled with clarity, growth, and endless possibilities. The power of elimination is in your hands—use it wisely and watch your life transform.

Disclaimer

The content of this book is intended for informational and educational purposes only and is not a substitute for professional medical advice, diagnosis, or treatment. The practices and strategies outlined are based on the author's personal experiences and research and are shared with the hope of providing useful insights and inspiration for readers seeking to eliminate bad habits and relationships in order to reduce stress and anxiety.

However, the decision to implement any of the suggestions or strategies presented in this book is solely the reader's responsibility. Individual outcomes may vary, and the author makes no guarantees regarding the effectiveness of these practices for any specific individual. The author and publisher disclaim any responsibility for any adverse effects or consequences that may arise from the use or application of the information contained herein. For personalized advice and support, especially if you are experiencing severe stress or anxiety, please consult a qualified mental health professional.

The stories mentioned in this book are fictional, and all characters are fictional as well. Any resemblance to actual persons, living or dead, or events is purely coincidental.

References

Chapter 1: Information Overload

1. Carr, N. (2011). The Shallows: What the Internet Is Doing to Our Brains. W. W. Norton & Company.
   This book explains how the internet and constant consumption of information affect our mental processes and overall well-being.
2. McGonigal, J. (2015). SuperBetter: A Revolutionary Approach to Getting Stronger, Happier, Braver, and More Resilient. Penguin Books.
   Offers insights into how digital distractions can drain our mental energy and how to overcome them.
3. Clear, J. (2018). Atomic Habits: An Easy & Proven Way to Build Good Habits & Break Bad Ones. Avery.
   A highly regarded resource on habit formation, including strategies for eliminating distractions and improving focus.
4. Newport, C. (2016). Deep Work: Rules for Focused Success in a Distracted World. Grand Central Publishing.
   Discusses the challenges of information overload and strategies for managing focus and productivity.
5. Santos, L. (2018). The Science of Well-Being. Coursera, Yale University.
   Highlights how our pursuit of excessive information does not necessarily contribute to happiness and well-being.
6. Turkle, S. (2015). Reclaiming Conversation: The Power of Talk in a Digital Age. Penguin Books.
   Provides research on how constant digital communication contributes to cognitive overload and reduces meaningful interactions.
7. McChesney, C., Covey, S. R., & Huling, J. (2012). The 4 Disciplines of Execution: Achieving Your Wildly Important Goals. Free Press.
   Covers effective time management strategies and avoiding distractions in a fast-paced, information-heavy world.
8. Historical Context on Knowledge Sharing:
   Discussed in Chapter 1 to illustrate humanity's evolution from limited, meaningful information-sharing to today's overwhelming influx of data

Chapter 2: Food & Fitness

1. Willpower as a Muscle:
   Baumeister, Roy F., and John Tierney. Willpower: Rediscovering the Greatest Human Strength. Penguin Books, 2012.
   This book delves into the concept of willpower, treating it as a limited resource that diminishes with repeated use, aligning with the idea presented in the chapter that willpower gets fatigued throughout the day.
2. Chakravyuha as a Metaphor for Modern Living:
   Devdutt Pattanaik. Jaya: An Illustrated Retelling of the Mahabharata. Penguin India, 2010.
   This source discusses the ancient Indian epic Mahabharata, where the concept of Chakravyuha is used as a metaphor for the complexities and entrapments of modern life.
3. Processed Foods and Their Impact on Mood:
   Gundry, Steven R. The Plant Paradox: The Hidden Dangers in "Healthy" Foods That Cause Disease and Weight Gain. Harper Wave, 2017.
   Gundry highlights how processed foods can negatively affect both physical health and mood, reinforcing the idea that dietary choices directly impact mental and physical energy.
4. Exercise and Nutrition Interactions:
   Lieberman, Daniel. The Story of the Human Body: Evolution, Health, and Disease. Vintage, 2014.
   This book emphasizes how evolutionary biology affects our modern habits, including the interaction between exercise and diet, much like the chapter's discussion on the feedback loop between food and fitness.
5. Marketing Junk Food:
   Moss, Michael. Salt Sugar Fat: How the Food Giants Hooked Us. Random House Trade Paperbacks, 2014.
   The reference highlights how food companies exploit consumers' weakened willpower at specific times, such as after a long day, which is reflected in the chapter's commentary on junk food advertising.

Chapter 3: Relationships

1. The Role of Karma in Relationships
   Reference works on karma from Hindu philosophy or texts on spirituality, particularly how early life experiences shape future relationships.
2. The Power of Choice in Friendships
   Reference: Baumeister, R. F., & Leary, M. R. (1995). "The Need to Belong: Desire for Interpersonal Attachments as a Fundamental Human Motivation." Psychological Bulletin, 117(3), 497–529.
3. Toxic Family Dynamics
   Reference: Bradshaw, J. (1990). Family Secrets: What You Don't Know Can Hurt You. New York: Bantam Books.
   Reference: Bowen, M. (1978). Family Therapy in Clinical Practice. New York: Jason Aronson.
4. Breaking Away from Parental Expectations
   Reference: Kiyosaki, R. T., & Lechter, S. L. (1997). Rich Dad Poor Dad: What the Rich Teach Their Kids About Money That the Poor and Middle Class Do Not! Warner Books.
5. Sara's Journey to Independence
   Reference: Ryan, R. M., & Deci, E. L. (2000). "Self-determination Theory and the Facilitation of Intrinsic Motivation, Social Development, and Well-being." American Psychologist, 55(1), 68–78.

Chapter 4: Money

1. Ramsey, D. (2003). The Total Money Makeover: A Proven Plan for Financial Fitness. Thomas Nelson.
   Provides practical advice on budgeting, debt elimination, and achieving financial freedom.
2. Sethi, R. (2009). I Will Teach You to Be Rich. Workman Publishing.
   Offers strategies for smart spending, effective investing, and building sustainable wealth.
3. Robin, V., & Dominguez, J. (2008). Your Money or Your Life: Transforming Your Relationship with Money and Achieving Financial Independence. Penguin Books.
   Discusses the philosophy of mindful spending and aligning money management with personal values.
4. Santos, L. (2018). The Science of Well-Being [Online Course]. Yale University, Coursera.
   Explores the concept of time affluence and well-being as primary drivers of happiness over wealth.
5. Taleb, N. N. (2007). The Black Swan: The Impact of the Highly Improbable. Random House.
   Provides insights into preparing for rare, unpredictable crises and the importance of decentralizing resources.
6. Fidelity Investments. (n.d.). "Debt Snowball vs. Debt Avalanche: Which Debt Payoff Strategy Is Right for You?"
   Explains methods for systematically eliminating debt and building financial stability.
7. McKinsey Global Institute. (2020). The Future of Work After COVID-19.
   Offers insights on economic shifts and financial resilience in a post-pandemic world.
8. Case Study: Tata Group's Diversification Strategy.
   Used as an example of balancing focused efforts with diversification for financial sustainability and resilience.

Chapter 5: Work

1. Pink, D. H. (2009). Drive: The Surprising Truth About What Motivates Us. Riverhead Books.
Provides insights into intrinsic motivation and how it shapes the modern workplace, emphasizing the transition from manual to knowledge-based work.
2. García, H., & Miralles, F. (2016). Ikigai: The Japanese Secret to a Long and Happy Life. Penguin Books.
Explores how the concept of Ikigai applies to finding purpose and fulfillment in work.
3. McKinsey Global Institute. (2020). The Future of Work After COVID-19.
Examines the impact of remote work and its implications for work-life balance and productivity
4. Newport, C. (2016). Deep Work: Rules for Focused Success in a Distracted World. Grand Central Publishing.
Discusses strategies for maintaining focus and productivity in an increasingly digital and remote work environment.
5. Harvard Business Review. (Various). Remote Work and Productivity.
Offers research and strategies on setting boundaries while working from home to maintain mental well-being and productivity.
6. Santos, L. (2018). The Science of Well-Being [Online Course]. Yale University, Coursera.
Provides a perspective on the psychological impact of work-life balance and prioritizing well-being over productivity.
7. Fried, J., & Hansson, D. H. (2010). Rework. Crown Publishing Group.
Challenges conventional notions of work and offers practical insights on redefining productivity and success.

Chapter 6: Time Affluence

1. Santos, L. (2018). The Science of Well-Being [Online Course]. Yale University, Coursera.
    Explores the importance of time affluence and its relationship to happiness and well-being.
2. Csikszentmihalyi, M. (1990). Flow: The Psychology of Optimal Experience. Harper & Row.
    Discusses the concept of the flow state and how time management contributes to optimal productivity and satisfaction.
3. Robinson, J. P., & Godbey, G. (1997). Time for Life: The Surprising Ways Americans Use Their Time. Penn State University Press.
    Analyzes time usage and its implications for modern life.
4. Fried, J., & Hansson, D. H. (2010). Rework. Crown Publishing Group.
    Provides a business-oriented perspective on managing time and avoiding unnecessary distractions.
5. Hsee, C. K., Zhang, J., & Wang, J. (2010). "Magnitude, Time, and Happiness: Discounting the Relevance of Delayed Consumption." Psychological Science, 21(5), 489–493.
    Researches time perception and its impact on happiness.
6. Ariely, D. (2008). Predictably Irrational: The Hidden Forces That Shape Our Decisions. HarperCollins.
    Examines how people perceive time and make decisions that influence productivity and satisfaction.
7. Clear, J. (2018). Atomic Habits: An Easy & Proven Way to Build Good Habits & Break Bad Ones. Avery.
    Offers practical strategies for using time effectively by building positive habits.
8. Einstein, A. (1916). Relativity: The Special and General Theory.
    Introduced the concept of time relativity, explaining how time and space interact.
9. Miralles, F., & García, H. (2016). Ikigai: The Japanese Secret to a Long and Happy Life. Penguin Books.
    Discusses how aligning your life with purpose (Ikigai) impacts time management.
10. Kahneman, D. (2011). Thinking, Fast and Slow. Farrar, Straus, and Giroux.

Explores cognitive biases and how they affect decision-making, including time-related decisions

REFERENCES

Chapter 7: Anything in Excess

1. Chanakya Neeti (Ancient Text).
   Cited for the Sanskrit verse: "अति रूपेण वै सीता चातगिर्वेण रावण:। अतदिानाद् बलर्िबद्धो ह्यति सर्वत्र वर्जयेत्।" It emphasizes the dangers of excess in beauty, arrogance, and generosity.
2. The Ramayana (Translated by R. K. Narayan).
   Referenced for the tale of Sita's beauty and Ravana's downfall, illustrating how extremes can lead to ruin.
3. The Paradox of Choice: Why More Is Less by Barry Schwartz (2004). Harper Perennial.
   Discusses how excessive choices can lead to decision fatigue and dissatisfaction, aligning with the chapter's theme of avoiding extremes.
4. Willpower: Rediscovering the Greatest Human Strength by Roy F. Baumeister & John Tierney (2011). Penguin Books.
   Explores the role of self-discipline in maintaining balance and avoiding excess in habits and life.
5. The Bible: Teachings on the Seven Deadly Sins.
   Used to discuss Christian doctrines about the dangers of excess, particularly gluttony, pride, and greed.
6. The Life-Changing Magic of Tidying Up: The Japanese Art of Decluttering and Organizing by Marie Kondo (2014). Ten Speed Press.
   Referenced to highlight how physical and mental clutter can result from excessive accumulation
7. Real-Life Example: Shul Kumar's Story.
   Cited to demonstrate how sudden excess wealth can lead to mismanagement and eventual downfall, as seen with the Indian "Kaun Banega Crorepati" winner.
8. Predictably Irrational: The Hidden Forces That Shape Our Decisions by Dan Ariely (2008). HarperCollins.
   Examines how individuals often fail to make rational decisions when overwhelmed by options or excess.
9. The Tale of King Bali (Hindu Mythology).
   Referenced to illustrate how extreme generosity without boundaries can lead to exploitation and self-destruction.

Chapter 8: Addition

1. Clear, J. (2018). Atomic Habits: An Easy & Proven Way to Build Good Habits & Break Bad Ones. Penguin Random House.
Used for the framework on habit formation, including the "cue-routine-reward" cycle and actionable strategies for building sustainable habits.

2. Duhigg, C. (2012). The Power of Habit: Why We Do What We Do in Life and Business. Random House.
Provides insights into how habits are created and reprogrammed, directly relevant to replacing negative patterns with constructive ones.

3. Peterson, J. B. (2018). 12 Rules for Life: An Antidote to Chaos. Random House Canada.
Explores fundamental principles for personal development, such as taking responsibility, incremental growth, and adding structure to life. Specifically relevant to building order and discipline through new habits.

4. Kondo, M. (2014). The Life-Changing Magic of Tidying Up: The Japanese Art of Decluttering and Organizing. Ten Speed Press.
Marie Kondo's decluttering principles inform the discussion on making space in life for meaningful additions.

5. Baumeister, R. F., & Tierney, J. (2011). Willpower: Rediscovering the Greatest Human Strength. Penguin Books.
Explains the role of self-control and willpower in maintaining new habits.

6. Heath, C., & Heath, D. (2010). Switch: How to Change Things When Change is Hard. Crown Business.
Discusses environmental design and its impact on behavior change, which aligns with mindful habit-building.

7. Santos, L. (2021). The Science of Well-Being [Online course]. Yale University.
Provides psychological foundations for creating positive habits and promoting well-being.

8. Kahneman, D., Krueger, A. B., Schkade, D., Schwarz, N., & Stone, A. A. (2004). "A Survey Method for Characterizing Daily Life Experience: The Day Reconstruction Method." Science, 306(5702), 1776–1780.
Offers insights on time perception and allocation, which supports mindful use of time after eliminating distractions.

9. Edison, T. A.

Example of Thomas Edison's iterative process of learning from failure and persistence, illustrating the importance of "failing fast" when testing new additions.